FROM MONK
TO PUNK
TO PUBLIC HEALTH

LESSONS LEARNED FOR AN
UNCERTAIN WORLD AHEAD

STEPHEN F MURPHY

Cover image by: Ink Sharia Creative Studio
Book design by: SWATT Books Ltd

Printed in the United Kingdom
First Printing, 2022

ISBN: 979-8-9873735-0-7 (Paperback)
ISBN: 979-8-9873735-1-4 (eBook)

Stevemuse Publishing
Silver Spring, MD USA

www.monktopunk.com

CONTENTS

Chapter 1: Early Years **5**
    Baby Catherine   5
    St Wilfrid's   6
    Mum & Dad   9
    Chemistry Calling   12

Chapter 2: Pastoral Beginnings **17**
    Mini Monk   17
    Living My Vows   20
    Two Years Off   26

Chapter 3: From Monk to Punk **31**
    College Music   31
    Finding the Arts   40
    London Land   44
    The Half Moon Theatre   49
    America in Sight   56
    Labour London   58

Chapter 4: A Great Escape **63**
    The Sizzle of Self   63
    Cidade Maravilhosa!   67
    At Sea   78

Chapter 5: A New Land **95**
    Radio Calling   95
    The Media Network   106
    Children's Health – A National Media Campaign   111

Chapter 6: It All Relates **119**
    Marriage in Heaven   119
    Understanding Relationships   121
    Berkeley Springs   127
    Separation   131
    Something in Common   134

Chapter 7: Learning From Life **137**
    Passion   137
    Selling Health   141
    Life's Lessons   145

Dedications **157**

Acknowledgements & Notes **159**

CHAPTER 1:
EARLY YEARS

Baby Catherine

Baby Catherine died in 1957 when she was ten months old of a hole in her heart. She was my baby sister and the source of my emotional hole, self-doubt, and need for approval. Before Catherine was born, I was a happy-go-lucky two-year-old, often amusing in play and talk. As the second child, I had attention from my parents and a built-in playmate in my brother, a year older. Yet baby Catherine's illness robbed me of my mother's attention as she took care of Catherine, who needed feeding every two hours. One day I said to my mother, "Don't feed that baby Mummy." Little did I know that one day baby Catherine would not need feeding anymore.

As Catherine's illness progressed, I went from being a contented child to one who sulked and was moody. My older brother Bernard seemed to have escaped the emotional deprivation I felt, perhaps having sated his emotional

L-R Bernard, Mum, Baby Catherine, Dad, author

needs by being born before me and having parental attention all to himself. It felt like the entire locus of deprivation, a feeling of being ignored, fell upon me. As baby Catherine was being fed, I hid. I hid in the corners of the house to find my comfort, my own space, and find an inner emotional connection. Hiding also offered a chance to set off worry bells in my mother as she frantically hunted the house for me. "Stephen, where are you?" she would cry out, to which my response was, "What me doing?" This was as though to say to my mother, what am I doing that would cause you to question my hiding? Guilt set in at an early age. So did my need to seek approval for what I did. If I was not going to receive attention, I would set out on a path to create my own place and be independent. If my parents had no time for me, only for my sick sister, I needed to be self-sufficient, entertain myself, and learn by listening rather than speaking until I could find a place in life I could call my own.

Baby Catherine was buried in the city graveyard. While her death was a blow to our family, it was, however bitter-sweet for me, a chance for me to come into my own again and welcome a new baby sister born two years later. Life edged back to normal, but the hole in Catherine's heart also left scars in my heart, scars that would need healing in ways I would later discover.

St Wilfrid's

That Monday morning in 1959 was a new beginning for me. It had been two years since baby Catherine died, two years for me to come out from my hidey holes and face the big world. I was standing on the kitchen table wearing a brown coat. My gloves were tied with a ribbon that my mother had carefully threaded from sleeve to sleeve across the shoulders to avoid me losing them. I wore brown shoes. I was five, and my mother was getting me ready for my first day at school. I was three feet tall so standing on the kitchen table made it easier for her to give me top-to-toe treatment. My brother stood alongside me. At six years old, he had one year more experience of school life than I did. We didn't speak; I assumed he just knew everything, he usually did. My brother was brilliant, always reading, but never a show-off. I was nervous. I had no experience of being outside the home for any length of time. My days of hiding had made me shy. My quietness earned me the title of the 'dark sheep' of the family.

We were a family of five children. My brother Bernard was a year older than me. My sister Mari was born in 1959 at home. Her given name was Marie Bernadette in homage to Lourdes, the town in southwest France that became known for apparitions of our Lady. Mari showed a streak of independence when, during her early teenage years, she dropped the 'e' from Marie and simply became Mari. My brother Sean came next in 1962, followed by my youngest sister Clare in 1967.

The kitchen was simple – yellow walls, a wooden table with red legs, and a hatch that passed from the kitchen through to the dining room. The hatch provided a portal to pass food from the kitchen to the dining room. In the late 1950s, besides a kitchen radio, a kitchen hatch was the latest

Dad with head in hatch looking at author

in-home innovation. I remember my father knocking a hole in the wall to create the hatch. My mother nervously watched as he swung the hammer to punch bricks through the wall. There was no room for a mistake, no money for outside help.

We lived on Lismore Road near Meersbrook Park, an area close to the industrial part of Sheffield but close enough to this park that overlooked the best of Sheffield, a steel city known for its manufacture of stainless steel cutlery. Our knives, our neighbour's forks, and everyone's dinner set was made close to our house. Every Sheffield wedding present was a boxed set of Sheffield cutlery. Everywhere you went, you could point to a knife and fork and turn it over to show it was made in Sheffield. I was proud of that. Yet this middle England city of half a million people would soon undergo a traumatic change, as Japan and other foreign manufacturers rapidly eclipsed its steel industry.

In Sheffield, we were remnants of a bygone age. We spoke Middle English, using pronouns like "thee" and "thou" in place of "you" and "yours". That was the dialect of South Yorkshire, the county in which Sheffield resides. We used terms like "Eeh by gum" to register surprise, "Shut thee gob" to silence a person and "Thart a reight mardy bum" at boys that were quiet and moody.

The hatch, the kitchen table, the brown coat, and my gloves meant everything to me – they were all I knew, my life inside the home. Today was a big day, I knew it, and my mother had me as prepared as she could, at least with neat clothes, hand-knitted gloves and hand-knitted scarf, balaclava, and knitted socks. My mother made everything for us. She knitted and sewed trousers and gloves. She would have made underwear, too if she could. My mother fretted over how she could afford to feed and clothe us. Her mother, who lived in Cork, Ireland, gave her sound advice – "All ye need to do is love them."

That morning I had a stomach full of porridge, and I was ready to go to my first day of school, prepared with clothes but not prepared for being outside the simple comfort of home, all

Havelock Bridge, Sheffield

I knew. Like a care package, I was delivered to the school. My father took us in his Morris Minor to Havelock Bridge to meet the school bus that would transport us to the Catholic school of St Wilfrid's. St Wilfrid's and its neighbourhood was posh compared to Lismore Road's rougher area.

Mum & Dad

I was raised in a Catholic household of Irish and Scottish stock. My mother, Mary Murphy, was Irish, born in Cork, the eldest of 12 children. They lived in a small house in Shandon, a district on the north side of Cork, near the river Lee. The house faced the church of St Anne and its famous bell tower.

Life in St Anne's, named after the church, was loud, as the twelve Drennan kids hustled around the dinner table to make sure they each got their fair share of food. You were assertive, or you starved. The eldest boy oversaw cutting the loaf of bread. My mother's father died of a heart attack in 1946. His health had declined, no doubt, due to being a prisoner in World War I. His death meant the older Drennan kids had to pitch in to keep house. As the oldest girl, Mum was expected to take on household duties from cooking to cleaning. That experience would later serve her well as a mother to two hungry boys and a father that had to walk eight miles to the school where he taught English. Mum left Ireland in 1948 to train

R - Mum with her father and siblings in Cork Ireland

as a nurse in England in the newly established National Health Service; her mother had asked her to stay but she had other plans.

My father, Frank Murphy, was born in Sheffield to a Scottish woman, May Cormack, who travelled to Sheffield for a position as a live-in housemaid. The close living quarters in the small house soon turned into a marriage to the master of the house, who therefore was to become my grandfather. The house where they lived and where my father grew up was on Tree Root Walk, now the site of the Royal Hallamshire Hospital. My grandmother was raised in a strict Victorian household where children didn't speak unless spoken to.

Such Victorian ways were not for my parents. My parents rarely hit us, excepting the occasional bottom slap, but teachers did. I received several blows to my hand from the headmistress's ruler for talking in the gym. I never understood why I was singled out because I don't remember talking. It felt unfair. I remained a quiet young boy after that. This would be the start of my undoing, the place where an offhand remark led to an unusual path.

We bought just the basics from the shops. My aunt and uncles, I assumed, were rich because they had fizzy drinks, sweets, and potted meat sandwiches with no crusts. While my aunts and uncles enjoyed the good life, at our dinnertime, we were treated to tripe, that ugly tasteless part of a sheep's stomach. Well, my parents ate tripe, which was the cheapest cut of meat, but they never forced us to eat it. We ate macaroni cheese and risotto, a fancy name for fried leftovers, or beef jelly and lard sandwiches. These food choices were cheap, and tastier than tripe and onions. I loved coming home to a feast of beef lard sandwiches with a helping of jellied beef juice. While today a snack like that may trigger a call from Children and Family Services, for us it was tasty and nutritious.

At school, a favourite break-time stop was the tuck shop, just a table and a teacher that would give us four blackjacks, a chewy treacle sweet, and four for a penny. It was a welcome reward for a morning's schoolwork.

Our Catholic upbringing brought with it the duties of the church: confession, first communion, stations of the cross, benediction, and of course, every Catholic's young boy's dream, to be an altar boy. I faced the challenge of my first confession at age seven. The boys and I assembled in Our Lady and St Thomas's pews and were reminded of our catechism and the Ten Commandments. Between the priest and our religious education handlers, we were encouraged to come to terms with everlasting life or the fires of Hades and so tell the truth about our sins in the hope that we may be forgiven. Now, at seven years old, coming up with a list of sins I had committed was a tricky business. I wasn't entirely clear what sin was except for a black mark on my soul. I knew I wouldn't care for that, yet as a first confession, I had to come up with at least a couple of sins to make the exercise worthwhile. We weren't provided with a cheat sheet of examples suitable for seven-year-olds, so as we each stepped into the confessional to bare our souls, it was up to our imagination to recite our sinful failings. I ate sugar out of the sugar bowl, I confessed to the priest, not being entirely clear if I had committed that sinful behaviour or even if eating sugar was a sin. With three Hail Marys and two Our Fathers, though, I was fully absolved from my sinful sugary encounters.

By completing my first confession and later my first communion, I was following every Catholic schoolboy's well-worn path to being an altar boy. Through successive kneeling experiences, I could ascend to the great honour of holding a candle during processions. One such procession was the annual Easter procession outside the church. Each of us pre-pubescent altar boys wore our vestments with pride, and we strode outside the church doors, following the priest as he headed toward Easter

Cross. I held my candle tightly. There was a light wind as I turned my head to see if Mum and Dad were watching me. As I turned, the flame of my candle brushed against the cassock of the altar boy in front of me. Time appeared to slow down as I watched the flame light the boy's cassock. My sense of wonder quickly abated as the priest recognising what might have been the first flaming processional altar boy, asked for someone to run to the church and bring a bowl of holy water to douse the flames. That was the height of my altar boy career, as my candle-carrying duties were quickly extinguished.

When I was 11, we moved closer to school from the Meersbrook area of Sheffield to the swankier Ecclesall area. We moved in 1966, the year England won the World Cup. All the stars aligned that year.

Chemistry Calling

Chemistry was on the standard curriculum at school but also proved to be a chance to test for the unexpected. In Sheffield in the early 1960s, procuring concentrated hydrochloric and sulphuric acid was a simple matter of asking for a sample from school or buying a small vial from the chemist on Bank Street. Sulphur, bromine, calcium carbide and many other base chemicals were well within reach of the average ten-year-old with an inquisitive mind. And so began our early experimentations into the unexpected consequences of chemical reactions. The sixties' illicit substances? These were ours!

My brother Bernard's and my ideas were legion. What would happen if you poured a mixture of hydrochloric and sulphuric acid down the drain on the road outside our house? Is there an interesting effect on a school uniform if you carry an open bottle of bromine in your inside blazer pocket? Calcium carbide mixed with water gives off inflammable acetylene gas. What then is the effect of mixing this compound inside a snowball and then lighting and throwing the flaming snowball? Our young minds were hungry for such knowledge!

No details of experiments were documented in the manner of thesis, method, result or conclusion, the standard scientific notation at the time. However, each experiment did hold a special place for us and a small coterie of equally imaginative and playful friends. I suspect but have no proof that our experiments were documented by the local fire brigade, perhaps in a tips-for-parents manual about why kids with scientific interests should not be left alone in the house or wander the streets carrying concealed test tubes. So let us explore these experiments, which I do want to remind the reader were conducted well before 9/11, so have no fear that there is some lurking terrorist training going on, merely inquisitive boys from over 50 years ago.

So, for our first experiment, Bernard, our friend Mark, and I, carefully carried two test tubes of concentrated acids down the street to a safe distance from the family house. We did not want what we assumed to be an exciting gaseous reaction to be in any way associated with the otherwise tidy, well-mannered, polite, short-clipped hair, Catholic boys that we were. We marched down the street, checking drains for opportune holes, persistent smells, or vapours of any sort. Our goal was a reaction to a chemical action, to something that could be heard, a bubbling, a fusion of deeper dredges and, of course, the resulting smells that might draw our neighbours' attention. As we slowly poured each test tube of acid down the drain into the public water supply (but that concern never crossed our minds), we could hear the gurgling sounds and the bubbling from the nether depths and the strong whiffs that ensued. What utter joy! We looked at each other and laughed, knowing that our experiment had worked! We had caused wonderful chaos in the pipes far beneath us. That was enough to know, and so on we walked down the street, content that we had been the cause of change below our feet.

Flaming snowballs is a rather novel concept and one that crept up on Bernard and me after we had experimented with calcium carbide and water. Calcium carbide is a whitish grey stone, like gravel. It is innocuous in look, like a simple mixture of small stones, yet noxious in every other way. This chemical came in a small cardboard tube. We bought about a pound in weight from the chemist – looking back, what on earth did he think we wanted it for, and why didn't he interrogate us? Our first tests were to pour an inch or two of plain water into a jam jar and add the calcium carbide. Acetylene has no smell, so when you first add water, all you see is some frothing, which was somewhat of a let-down, almost a failure in our eyes. The fun started when you added fire to the mixture in the form of a lighted match. Lighting a jam jar that exuded a flammable gas did not seem to offer the level of control we sought and might be dangerous. We wanted danger, but only controllable danger! Where we could find control was an old medicine bottle with a pinhole punched through the top. The gas would then come out of the pinhole and provide, when lit, a continuous but controlled blue acetylene flame. Bernard and I looked at each other keenly, knowing that we had almost reached chemical nirvana. However, there was more experimental work to be done.

With a foot of snow on the ground and the simple deduction that snow was simply frozen water, we realised that we could take our experiment one step further by trying a new angle. That was the essential beauty of calcium carbide – it is an inflammable stone which you can bury inside a snowball. The snow surrounding the chemical will melt, giving off gas which you can then set alight. It took some dexterity to get the timing right. The key was not to be holding a flaming snowball for too long before you launched it. Genius, it worked!

We had one more trick up our sleeves, though, after discovering that the cement holding the railings by Meersbrook Park Rd contained sulphur. Sulphur, when lit, produces a small, almost invisible blue flame giving off a choking gas – sulphur dioxide which smells like bad cabbage. With matches in hand, we lit the base of each railing, thus enveloping the surrounding area. We didn't wait to see if parkgoers noticed.

Emboldened by these creative chemical calculations, we continued our elemental endeavours throughout our schooling. From these humble but formative scientific experiments, my brother Bernard went on to eventually obtain a PhD in nuclear physics from Oxford University, although, thankfully, treating the nuclear reaction with a little more gravitas than water and calcium carbide. This early love of chemistry helped me to choose to go on to take and pass chemistry A level as well as A level physics at Cambridge College of Arts and Technology.

We learned a great deal and only suffered one humiliating defeat. One afternoon, when our parents were out of the house, Bernard and I set ourselves loose in the cellar and concocted every possible combination of substances, pouring toxic mixtures into every hole in the concrete floor of the basement. Into and around each hole, we stuffed rolled-up newspaper scraps and lit each one with a match. The paper smouldered, and the holes bubbled, each giving off its own unique flavour of gas. Unbeknownst to us, smoke was starting to fill the cellar and seep into the house upstairs. When Mum returned home, she opened the front door and was overcome by a thick fog of smoke. She immediately called the fire brigade, and within minutes large men in black and yellow came thundering into the house and down into the cellar. It was all smoke and no fire but still a moment to be summoned to the living room and firmly dressed down by the chief fire officer. Warnings of dire consequences, the safety of our mother, the house, and even the entire street rang through our ears. That was the last time Bernard and I performed chemistry experiments together, but to this day, it remains a common tie that binds us, our chemical bond.

CHAPTER 2:
PASTORAL BEGINNINGS

Mini Monk

In 1968 I was 13 and this was when I made the first conscious decision about the direction my early life was going to take. At this precocious, pre-pubescent age, I decided to become a monk. Well, that is not the term the holy order used in reference to its members. This had nothing to do with the sixties, but the term applied to the habitually dressed men who wore habits; full-length black robes with a white neck collar, a holy hominoid, was 'Brother'.

This religious order was founded in Rheims in 1680 by a Frenchman by the name of St. John Baptist De La Salle. Translated, this means 'Of the Room'. At thirteen, with a modicum of the French language behind me, I paid no attention to the absurdity of the name. Everyone in my English Catholic high school, which was also named 'De La Salle,' used the name with free abandon. For me, at 13, it seemed like a straightforward name for a religious order, and I didn't care too much what they called the school. As young but oh so clever schoolboys, we had established our own pre-teen, derogatory, but inventive vocabulary for the name of the school and the teachers.

The holy order's founder, Monsieur De La Salle, had the idea that he would form a band of noble teachers to teach the poor of Paris. Having conquered Paris, he moved on to Europe and then to England. Each Brother would take three vows: chastity, poverty, and obedience. With that sort of carnal discipline in place at the age of 13 and in this virtuous tradition, I set out to fulfil my righteous calling.

My parents, while devoted, did not bless my decision, but with four other mouths to feed and a sense that I was clear that this was the path I wanted to take, they unwillingly acceded to my stated vocation. My uncle Matt in Ireland had become a priest years before, and each time we visited Ireland, my grandmother spoke with loving pride of his priesthood calling. For me, this new journey was about recognition of who I was and who I was to become. It was also a chance to escape the glare of brilliance that emanated from my brother Bernard, a boy for whom reading the dictionary in bed or researching the possible Latin translation for car park were enjoyable pastimes. My teacher remarked to me one day in school, "You will have to work harder if you want to be as good as your brother." Such an undercutting remark was unfortunately all too common among our deprecating teachers who, in hindsight, suffered from a lack of self-worth. Perhaps because of this careless comment, I lacked confidence in my abilities, but that day, I set out determined to prove my worth, obtain my due recognition, and forge a different path in life.

Michael and I sat in the back of the van outside Midland train station in Sheffield and wondered what would become of us. We were 13-year-old boys who had chosen to join an order of Catholic brothers, go through three years of training and post-training, and take vows of chastity, poverty, and obedience. It was 1968 and our decision to move away from home, bypass a typical school life for a country life devoid of girls, for a distant novitiate, at the time seemed normal for the day. I had left home before to go to school, but this day was different. I would be leaving home for months.

My suitcase rested by my feet, its bluish colour reminding me of our blue-tinged kitchen and the comforts and family I was about to leave behind. I looked at the soot-covered walls of the Midland station, knowing this was to be the last sight of Sheffield I would see for a while. It was a grey overcast September day, and I could smell the familiar odour of industry that pervaded Sheffield at the time – a smell of steel factories, of molten hot furnaces, and the acrid whiff from the train station that still hosted the remnants of coal-powered steam trains. It was the smell of home, a home I would be leaving behind for a new life and a new journey.

The evening before leaving home, we enjoyed a family meal together, my last for many months. I had spent my savings on an LP recording of *The Jungle Book*, a Disney-animated film of Rudyard Kipling's short stories. Perhaps it was prescient that I imagined I was going to be delivered into the jungle of life, a Mowgli, not a Murphy, a mere cub of a boy heading out on a moral purpose – to understand myself. The Jungle Book song, 'The Bare Necessities', ran as an essential theme through my home life, but for me, the journey had another theme song from the Disney film, finding 'My Own Home.' That LP and those songs became a legend in my family, a parable for my new beginning.

Brother Dominic opened the driver's door and waved cheerily to us both and asked if we were looking forward to the journey south to the Brothers' training school, The Juniorate. During a recruitment visit to Sheffield's De La Salle high school, Brother Dominic had presented us with a glossy brochure containing black and white pictures of boys tending gardens and playing table tennis. Catholic missionaries had also visited my former school the year before and told us about South America and their work in exotic places to teach the locals about religion. Their Catholic faith was all I knew; it was familiar and right because my parents practised it devotedly. We attended Mass every Sunday and Benediction on Wednesday evenings. My parents were right to attend church. Brother Dominic was right to have recruited us. We were right in the decision that led us to be sitting in that van that Saturday afternoon. The image of school life the brothers offered was seductive and, in my young mind, a romantic fairy tale opportunity too. Mine was not so much a spiritual journey but a journey to a land I could call my own.

We set off for St. Cassian's Kintbury, a manor house set deep in the heart of Berkshire, England, near Kintbury, an old village in the Kennet Valley located between Hungerford and Newbury. The manor house was built in the late 16th century in the English county of West Berkshire. The house was given the name 'Saint Cassian's' after a Roman martyr who was a teacher and was venerated by De La Salle. The location was as far away from Sheffield as I had ever been, and its pastoral setting was designed to keep teenage boys focused on Mass, the rosary and manual labour and away from traditional teenage pursuits. It was far from any females but rather close to rats, though, which roamed the school grounds with free abandon. So, St Cassian's polished wooden floors, rambling stairs, scary dormitories and hidden rooms is where I spent my formative years.

Living My Vows

When I was not studying, singing in the chapel choir, or reciting the rosary as I walked through the grounds each morning, I was undertaking manual labour.

Manual labour was just the Brothers' way of saying that life was hard. Each morning, after a silent breakfast, we each walked from the dining hall refectory to our labour assignment. Assignments could be easy and fun or gruelling and tough. It was hard stooping down to pick potatoes in the vegetable garden. It was not fun cleaning toilets. If you got polishing machine duty, polishing the wooden floors in the grand hallway, you were on an ultimate pleasure trip and had a powerful buffering machine to use. Hidden in a corridor behind the boys' toilets was a room full of tins of bright orange wax. Armed with a very large tin of aromatic floor wax and a powerful machine and no supervision, for a 13-year-old boy, this was nearly nirvana.

The entrance hall was rarely used, except by the Brothers who used it as a passage between their private dining area and the chapel. Of course, 17th-century wooden planks with a quarter-inch layer of wax neatly buffed until the wax was transparent would be treacherous for anyone. Brothers had a special challenge, though, because

Author in picture centre in blazer in St Cassians Chapel with Brother Damian

their everyday clothing was a long black cassock, an ankle-length cotton or woollen robe. The origin of the word cassock is thought to come from the word Cossack, a nomad and adventurer known for a crouched positioned wild leg dance. The term ankle-length is, of course, not precise as to measurement, so the chance of the robe becoming caught up with feet instead of ankles was quite high. I never witnessed a Brother-to-floor event, but my morning hard labour made the dreams sweeter.

From this pastoral countryside retreat, I could ponder upon the vows I had promised to take when I would later ascend to the seniorate class, the one following my current attachment to the juniorate: chastity, poverty, and obedience.

At 13, of course, chastity lacked meaning for me. I had experienced the growth of pubic hair but had little idea of the reason behind this unexpected nether region sprouting. My high school teacher had tried to warn me before I left to join the Brothers about the potential problems I might encounter a total adherence to a chaste lifestyle. Still, at 13, with no immediate background in the rules governing 'lifestyles', I paid little heed to his cautionary utterances.

We slept in dormitories, each named after saints. Mine was St Joseph's. By all historical accounts, St Joseph was a mild-mannered man and I, as a mild-mannered young boy, felt honoured to be sleeping under his watch. Yet my tranquil exterior masked a curious mind. I bought luminous gum on a trip to Newbury, the local market town. I had had prior experience with luminous gum during the time my brother and I had performed chemistry experiments. I knew the gum would melt when exposed to heat. The dormitory was surrounded wall to wall in exposed hot water pipes, a perfect surface to experiment. One afternoon, I walked between the beds and pasted luminous gum on every hot water pipe in St Joseph's. Within minutes after lights out, a ghostly apparition surrounded 25 boys, a sign from heaven that St Joseph was watching over us. The lights were out, but it was showtime for the shy and a chance to peer upon the quiet masturbators. No one found out my luminous secret.

Author front center with trainee brothers at St Cassians

Yet my crime was slight compared to the boys that lit weighted bangers (firecrackers) in the water-filled bathroom sinks. The firework explosion blew out the bottoms of the sinks. Another firework trick I learned was to place a lighted banger in an empty milk churn. The resulting sonorous boom must have woken St Cassian and St Joseph from eternal sleep.

While I was not called to account for these mischievous events, the head Brother did call each of us into his study each month for a quiet talk about life. Brother Joseph carefully placed the student's chair so that it aligned with a thin bead of light that came through the study's curtains. This was, of course, a classic interrogation approach, in that I could barely make out Brother Joseph's face, yet mine was flooded with a blinding light. Innocent questions about how I was doing in my studies or how my parents were seemed to take on a darker meaning.

Poverty was merely a word, not an idea understood. My parents had seen to it that the word poverty would remain just as a term in my vocabulary, not as a lived experience. We were not poor, but neither were we rich. My parents lived on teacher and nursing salaries which were barely enough to feed five kids. In the 50 years since, shamefully, the relative wages for teachers and nurses have not sufficiently improved.

One summer, while I was away, Dad sold World Books Encyclopaedia door to door to help pay for a family holiday in the Isle of Man. Not being steeped in sales practices, he nonetheless recited the 'overcoming objections' such as "I cannot afford a leather-bound set of encyclopaedias"; "I have three kids to feed and clothe". As with all good encyclopaedia-selling operations, there was always an answer provided by the corporate sales trainers for such feeble excuses. Dad sold enough of the books for us to have a new carpet and a holiday. We also had a car. So, I knew little about poverty because of my father's hard work during his precious summer holidays and other parental endeavours.

While I knew nought about poverty, I did know about obedience. I knew the word, and, like all children of that age, I had a fair grounding in the concept. I was a moody child, at odds with my siblings and parents on many occasions. To their great credit, given the era in which we were brought up, my parents rarely hit us except for the occasional slapped bottom. Instead, they employed a sternness of demeanour and attitude. Their faces and tone were enough to communicate the seriousness of the situation and their disapproval of our conduct. There was never any threat, but somehow, through this firm but not severe upbringing, we obeyed.

While the rosary and religious obedience were de rigueur, some of the brothers had more progressive ideas, and in rather startling recognition of the changing times, took a group of us to see, of all the West End shows they could have chosen, the newly-opened musical *Hair*. Yes, that's right, the show complete with a free-love message, a brief nude scene, a depiction of the use of illicit drugs and a denigration of the American flag, all celebrating the dawning of the Age of Aquarius. This oh-so 1960s theatrical event, which still had the power to shock in a revival 50 years later, triggered in me and everyone who went (probably including the senior Brothers too!), judging from us boys' wide-eyed comments to each other afterwards, a sexual dawning and an awakening to a heady cocktail of obedience- and chastity-testing ideas! There is the mixed-up, tumultuous decade that was the 1960s summed up in that one rather mad event – a still (outside of theatre and the tiny enclave that was the reality of Swinging London) buttoned-up Britain colliding head-on with a glimpse of the freedoms to come.

I had one favourite teacher, Brother Damian, who taught English and drama. It was drama that most appealed to me, allowing me to get lost in acting out The Beatles 'A Day in the Life'. Damian later produced us boys in *Oh What A Lovely War*, a satire on World War I, complete with risqué lyrics such as 'They Were Only Playing Leapfrog', the gay reference which I never understood at the time. Conversely, there were also regular forays in serious religious study and seminal practice which was somehow to be expected under the circumstances in which I found myself. Between these two extremes, radical was a word that began to develop a greater meaning for me.

Yet, of the three vows I was supposed to take in the seniorate, I could say with some honesty that in my early years, even post the Brothers, it was poverty that I chose to practise on regular occasions by dint of being skint. Adhering to chastity remained remarkably easy too at this time, although chance would have been a fine thing!! It seemed to be baked into my DNA despite the stirrings that *Hair* had created.

However, as my later teenage years took hold, it became clear that it was obedience that was not my strong suit. I found myself chafing against the confines of this religious calling. While I had, at times, been drawn to serious religious study and seminal practice, life as a mini monk had palled after five years. The initial idea of

Brother Joseph center, author to his left, light pants

teaching the poor and underprivileged would have been a logical extension of my calling to the Brotherhood, and it had held a perverse romanticism at 13. I had become cynical at the way the religious order had drifted from teaching the poor to becoming a basket for direct government grants. The Brothers' role became one of teaching the children of the middle class. Meanwhile, other publicly-funded schools were reserved for the less well-off. Now, though, at 18, having felt the temporal stirrings of manhood, the word 'radical' kept coming into my thoughts – the need to find a new, alternative path.

So, my life as a minor monk passed from 13 to 18 in English countryside retreats in Berkshire and then in Cambridge in East

Anglia. In this tranquillity, we were far from the Paris riots, 1960s music, and free love. Is that a note of regret? Not really... I studied like any ordinary school student and achieved O Level passes in maths, physics, chemistry, English language and French, and A Level passes in physics and chemistry while failing maths.

Two Years Off

Instead of going straight to college, in 1972, at 18 years old, I decided to take two years off to enter the world of work. Taking time off before entering college had become a fashionable thing to do, and I felt I would benefit from some work experience. This was my big transition from monkhood to early adult life. One thing mini monkhood had conferred on me was the need to do something to help others. I joined a London-based not-for-profit organisation called Community Service Volunteers (CSV) that placed young people in a variety of settings, paying them a small stipend for their volunteer efforts. Young people were recruited to work in hospitals and with the handicapped and underprivileged. My placement was in Carlton Hayes psychiatric hospital, in Narborough, near Leicester, where I was a volunteer nurse assistant. The idea was that each of us volunteers would have a minder from CSV who would guide us and rate us on our work. Somehow, the training aspect of volunteerism never quite worked out. Instead, we acted like any other nurse or admin assistant. I changed beds and learned the very practical 'hospital corners' method of neatly folding the sheets at the end of the bed.

It took something of a growth leap for me to make this transition from monasticism to volunteerism, but I found a path. It helped, too, to have at least carried over some pledges I would have made had I continued as a monk. Poverty was one. My weekly pay was seven pounds per week, £4 for my meals and £3 for lodging in the hospital's nursing staff wing.

I also learnt about the more controversial aspects of psychiatric nursing, like electric shock therapy. While it was not a requirement of my duties, in a shortage, I would be called upon to help hold down a patient undergoing shock treatment. Largactil and Mogadon were the drugs of choice in Castle Ward, the high-security ward where I worked. These were powerful pacifiers for the schizophrenic clientele.

They were all crazy, of course, the patients and, to maintain joie de vivre, the nurses. I recall one patient, Bill. Bill had a saying, oft repeated, that *Smoking Dullens the Senses and Tea Weakens the Ankles*. Bill knew stuff. He was a mathematician, a visionary.

The hospital was located near a farm. The story went that another patient, Bert, wandered away from the ward one afternoon and was seen later literally wrestling with a bull. Since Bert was well built, stocky, and endowed with the kind of strength that only comes from a complete lack of the powers of reason, the story went that Bert had the brawn and a sufficient lack of presence of mind to tackle the beast. Whether the details were entirely accurate, the story of Bert wrestling bulls pervaded the ward, and from then on, he received massive doses of pacifiers to prevent him from repeating his bull-wrestling episode.

Bert's subdued aggression took on the form of gentle affection. Because of the drugs, his otherwise forceful and facially directed fist movements were reduced to a gentle tap on the jaw as he passed by you. The role of the nurse was always to be pleasant to Bert. If Bert didn't want to do something, then no amount of coaxing could make him comply. Staff nurses sternly advised against getting on the wrong side of Bert.

One day I did get on Bert's wrong side and spent the rest of the afternoon scuttling through corridors trying to avoid his manic gaze and menacing pace toward me. While I was perturbed by the shock therapy treatment, I was thankful that Bert's true emotions and bodily strength had been medically muted.

By this time, it was October 1973; Edward Heath was Prime Minister, and we had just joined the European Common Market. Pink Floyd had just released their best-selling album *Dark Side of the Moon*, and the IRA's bombs had hit Oxford St, Sloane Square and Victoria Station.

Sometime during this period, I moved to Oxford and took a job with a freight train haulage firm. I was a labourer. My task was to unload trains of boxes and meat products destined for the supermarket shelves. I stayed in my brother Bernard's flat. By now, he was a student at Hertford College and studying physics. While the labourer job gave me an opportunity to experience Oxford and the exclusive Oxford University lifestyle, in Oxford parlance, 'Town and Gown', it was not a fulfilling occupation. I soon moved back to Leicester.

My term with CSV ended after six months, although I then put in a further round of nursing and social work, as though somehow to redeem myself for any later antisocial behaviour. Having been enamoured by hospital life, I looked for another nursing assistant job. If I qualified, I thought, I might become a state registered nurse like Mum. I found a job in a Leicester hospital as a care assistant. I also worked as a hospital cleaner. One day I entered a patient's room, not realizing she had just died. What was the protocol for room cleaning amidst death? I didn't know, but this episode contributed to me beginning to feel that I had done my time in healthcare.

I hadn't been at the hospital long before I was accepted for a position as a childcare officer at a children's home in Leicester. I continued my relationship with Community Service Volunteers, finding that its placements advanced my need to help others.

My employer was the city council. The home housed 12 children ranging in age from five to fifteen. The kids had all been taken into care because of family breakdowns, parents being in prison or because the social worker thought they needed supervision. My job was to care for them. My duties ranged from supervising meals to play activities and making sure the children went to bed, though I seemed to have no control over how quietly this routine occurred. I found the duties frustrating, as the kids just wouldn't follow my instructions. I seemed to have little control, and this frustration led me to start thinking about considering university and a degree once again. Perhaps something to do with social work – after all, I had spent the past two gap years engaging in some type of social work.

CHAPTER 3:
FROM MONK TO PUNK

College Music

I had assumed that my two years of the practical aspects of taking care of others would be treated as helpful to my proposed social work studies. However, when I applied, the social work course was full. The polytechnic careers office offered an alternative to social work in the form of housing management, a course that would train me in the management of Britain's public housing. I dutifully enrolled, hoping I would find some interest in these studies. However, while I found some courses engaging – property law, general law, (contracts and torts) economics, town planning and architectural drawing, courses on drains were of considerably less appeal. I had to look for alternative pursuits to gutter management. I found it in music.

I had been an avid fan of the DJ, John Peel, and would listen to his radio show anytime I could, to learn about upcoming bands. It was John Peel and Radio Caroline, the pirate radio station that broadcast from a ship in the North Sea, that had fulfilled the creative rebel in me. I had found an outlet. That link with Peel had continued after he joined the BBC in 1967, and by 1975, when I was 20 years old, he remained the champion of new and interesting music.

At a Bristol Polytechnic freshman fair in September 1975, held in the first week of college activities for new students, I signed up to help the student union organize entertainment activities. For any lover of music, this was a dream post, and yet there was no opposition to my nomination for the part-time post. So, I was duly elected unopposed to serve as site entertainments officer with the 'Ents team' on the campus where I studied. I continued with my drainage studies while serving in this unpaid position.

In the seventies, the main entertainment activity at most colleges and universities was the weekly disco, and Bristol was no exception. The one at my site on campus, Unity Street, generally attracted the largest crowd, often four or five hundred students. Within weeks I knew how to set up a disco system, complete with flashing lights and a stroboscope – professional stuff! I also became proficient at setting up the box office and collecting the door takings for these disco events. The Ents team at the Unity Street site soon developed into an efficient and oftentimes mobile force within the college community. We were frequently called upon to set up discos at other college locations.

At the time, there were just three full-time student union officers – a president, a treasurer, and an information officer. Sometime during my first year, the student union officers made an agreement with the polytechnic authorities for there to be seven full-time salaried student union officers. The positions were to cover president, treasurer, publicity and information, arts and entertainments, clubs and societies, services and education, and welfare. At the end of my first college year, I decided to leave my studies and run for the full-time position of Arts and Entertainments Officer. I had not found the housing course to be fulfilling and felt that the student union position would provide a one-time opportunity to enter a career in the entertainment business. At the time, I believed that this was one that would always survive under any economic circumstances, even war.

I wrote a manifesto, citing my experience and knowledge in student entertainment programming, plus I arranged hustings speeches and created election posters and leaflets – a whole campaign to achieve being voted onto this post. I won and became one of the few full-time student entertainment officers in the country. However, I was not content with simply promoting rock concerts and discos. I wanted to broaden the scope of my job by including performance art, theatre, film, antiracist events, and ethnic-oriented activities. I attended a conference for student entertainment officers where these new ideas were discussed.

The Unity Street and Coldharbour Lane student base consisted of Tory voting business students, a voter base that I could capture if I promised to lower the annual £2,000 Ents subsidy to £400, a move I felt confident that I could achieve because our disco enterprise of four very popular weekly events was minting money. During my second year, I was able to eliminate this subsidy completely, a move that was embraced by the business students who voted for me once again.

Having learned that there was more to life than discos, I put together my first freshers' entertainment programme for incoming students. The polytechnic had some 4,500 full-time and 3,500 part-time students, arranged on five college sites across Bristol. Besides choosing and promoting the programme, I was responsible for all the peripheral activities of budgeting, licensing, room bookings, timetabling and publicity, advertising, booking of acts and contract negotiations with performers. I had two weeks to fill the two opening weeks of the student year with activities every night. I planned two major rock concerts, a series of performance arts activities, a couple of film screenings, some group workshop activities as well as a heavy diet of discos. Some of these, though, were discos with a difference.

I had a local theatre company, the 'Crystal Theatre of the Saint', an experimental theatre company, a group from nearby Bath, come into the Unity Street campus and build a stage and backdrop. The company also arranged lighting and special stage effects. They donned wild costumes, interspersed themselves in the crowd, and brought exactly the kind of rebel creativity I craved.

I also hired the same theatre company to perform a lunchtime event in the cafeteria. I wanted this, and other theatre performances, to move the department away from a standard college fare of rock music and discos and, instead, provide a light-hearted and broader arts programme for the students.

So, the Crystal Theatre of the Saint duly arrived at the cafeteria, wearing dark suits and crepe masks over their faces, thus obscuring all facial features. Most students found their antics merely amusing. However, one handicapped and nervy new student nearly passed out in shock at the sight of a performer entering the lift she was in, in this wild garb. I spent the afternoon with her and a student counsellor, trying to mollify this traumatised student. I recognized that there were limits to how creative I could be and that I needed to be aware of the impact of the entertainment programme on others that were less inclined to embrace such wild and wacky expressionistic art.

I took the opportunity to spend my year as Arts and Ents Officer to get to know the music business. I befriended music agents at the various talent agencies like Cowbell, a top London-based music agency at the time, as well as the local Rainbow Entertainments agency run by Derek Barker and Adrian Squires. Musically, the mid-seventies were a turbulent era. While in 1975, it was appropriate to promote a concert by US West Coast rock bands like Country Joe and the Fish, suddenly, by 1977, the punk explosion had happened, and the hippyish West Coast sound was out, to be replaced by the likes of the hard and urgent sound of The Jam. It was the era of the Sex Pistols, who had blown the doors off the music scene and were storming England with their raucous brand of music. The Sex Pistols were inciting riots at venues throughout the country and promptly getting banned by city councils across the UK.

In this atmosphere, it was an exciting time to be promoting music concerts. And I had a 650-standing capacity hall at the Ashley Down campus to fill. For most events, this capacity was enough to recoup costs. However, for larger, and more popular visiting artists, like Al Stewart and Procol Harum, this 650-seat capacity hall was not enough to recoup costs and still charge a reasonable ticket price for students. That size group's fee was about £1,000 (about $1,750). So, in those instances, I was able to book the Colston Hall in Bristol, with its 2,000-seat capacity, owned and operated by the city council.

For the Procol Harum gig the band contract I received from his agent, Ian Copeland (whose younger brother is Stewart Copeland, the drummer in the Police), required me to hire and ship a Steinway piano from London to Bristol at considerable expense. Al Stewart had fewer contract

Author with Al Stewart, Birchmere, VA, US 2013

requirements though I did wonder what responsibility we had for what seemed like an endless supply of backstage drugs brought in by the band. I later saw Al Stewart at a concert in the Washington DC area, and I mentioned that I produced his *Year of the Cat* concert in Bristol in 1977. He kindly asked why we were not still working together.

During my two years as an arts and entertainment officer, I had the opportunity to book dozens of large and small rock and folk music acts. This included everyone from folk artist

Richard Thompson to The Tourists, Annie Lennox's forerunner to Eurythmics. I booked The Jam to appear on 11 June 1977 at Redland campus, with local punk band The Cortinas as the support act. The Cortinas had recently been signed by a record label and were Bristol's equivalent of the Clash. Guitarist Nick Sheppard later joined the Clash. I also booked the Flying Burrito Brothers, charging just £1.20 per ticket.

I was too nervous to book the Sex Pistols due to their and their audience's reputation. However, when I was offered a chance to book half the band, guitarist Steve Jones and bassist Glen Matlock, I jumped at the opportunity, hosting them at the Unity Street cafeteria. The gig quickly sold out and even though the ticket price was just 50p, we made a handsome profit. I was apprehensive at the potential for trouble, but none occurred. I also hosted the film *Jubilee*, which featured the Sex Pistols, on 29 November 1977, a Tuesday, which turned out to be a great way to increase bar takings on a weekday night.

Other bands I promoted at the students' union fell into the punk and new wave genre, bands like Radio Stars, an offshoot of Marc Bolan's early band John's Children. When the New York Dolls disbanded in 1975, guitarist Johnny Thunders and drummer Jerry Nolan formed the Heartbreakers. I was lucky enough to book them for the Freshers Ball alongside other New Wave bands like The Adverts, The Boys, and The Models. And a real coup, I also booked the Ramones, regarded as the original New York punk band. I announced our band line-up in Poly Ents fanzine D.O.P.E, Diary of Poly Ents. The masthead included a picture of a joint, as though that was the driving force for music in those days. To me, and it seemed to many, there was a feeling that music and dope hung together. Having said that, many of the punk bands favoured the opposite of dope, spurning its mellowing effects in favour of amphetamines like Speed. To show how quickly terms change, 'straight' in those days was a term for people that didn't smoke dope (pot), not a term for someone that wasn't gay.

I also promoted an antiracist reggae & jazz evening, and collaborated with student societies in film screenings and theatre programmes. One of the sabbatical officers, Tim Manning, had censured the entire sabbatical team for not following through on its support for gay students. In the mid-seventies, the LGBTQ+ community did not have the level of support they have today, but Tim was right, we should have done more to support the community of gay students. So, I then thought about ways I could support the community through the entertainments programme.

Fighting racism became another flashpoint on campus as we saw the rise of fascism, fuelled by the emergence of the National Front and stemming right back to the late 60s, with Enoch Powell's Rivers of Blood speech in the West Midlands and his rallying of London dock workers who feared that post-colonial immigration would take away their jobs. Most of the New Wave bands in the mid-to-late seventies were all white. To offset the whiteness, I hired an all-black band, whose name I now forget. In *Union News*, we also reprinted an interview with DJ, film director and musician Don Letts, who founded Big Audio Dynamite with Clash guitarist Mick Jones. Letts drew comparisons between reggae and black culture and punk, recognising that both were anti-establishment movements. As Letts explained, "Cause Johnny Rotten was telling me the other day, he's walking down the street now and the cops are hitting on him, takin' him into the van, trying to bust him 'cause of the way he looks. It's the same shit we go through, like with my hair and the red, gold, and green."

By the time we got to Bristol, we were half a million strong, well 8,000 anyway, so said the newspaper report of the Ashton Court Festival held on 5/6 August 1978. Given my position as social secretary I felt I could contribute to this newly-created music festival. I attended the meetings of the Bristol Community Free Festival, suggesting artists like Ricochets, Wreckless Eric and a steel band from Bath. The festival was disorganized, and the sound system performed poorly, but I could claim to have, if not the American Woodstock experience, its Bristol, England equivalent, and for me, that was good enough.

During this time, I learned some valuable, if basic, publicity skills such as copywriting and print production. This included collaborations with music agencies and record companies like Phonogram and Chrysalis Records.

The student union owned and managed a retail enterprise selling clothes, food, books and stationery items, plus ten bars and a travel bureau. The union also published a respected student newspaper called *Bacus*. Though the journal name approximated the Roman god of wine and fertility, its genesis probably had more to do with the Bristol area committee and union of students than any debauched references, however well-deserved. Through these related activities and union concerns, I became familiar with a variety of business issues beyond my immediate field of responsibility. I upgraded the disco audio and lighting equipment and hired a part-time person to manage a student equipment rental business and an equipment maintenance service. Through these activities and careful budgeting, during my first year as the elected student officer, as mentioned, I had been able to reduce the £2,000 entertainment subsidy (about £13,000 in today's money) to just £400, and then eliminate union subsidies altogether in favour of a profit-making entertainments enterprise. I used the subsidy allowances to allow us to stage various commercial arts and the so-called 'minority entertainments' events.

My successes during the first year contributed to the drafting of a competent manifesto and re-election to the post for a second year. I had booked two major bands, generated significant income from discos, and introduced novel entertainment programmes for their time.

However, after my second year in the role, I was burned out and wanted to leave college and enter the workplace. As a grand finale I produced a punk spectacular concert at Ashley Down in my final year, an event that would get us banned from future concerts at that venue. Halfway through the concert, we were attacked by a marauding group of young people, possibly football fans. Our modest front door entrance and security were no match for the violent gang who entered the concert hall throwing missiles of chairs and beer bottles. Quite apart from the concert ban, the violent event made me wonder if punk would be part of my future or if I should seek out gentler forms of entertainment. The mid-1970s in England were culturally complex. This was a time of mass strikes for better wages, creating the Winter of Discontent which would present a weakness in the Labour party that Margaret Thatcher, the newly elected leader of the Conservatives, could later exploit. Musically, the ground had shifted dramatically from laid-back West Coast rock and singable Beatles songs to the thrashing guitars, harsh sounds and angry lyrics of punk. Yet I saw value in my role in the world of entertainments, and I now saw a place for using entertainments and the arts within the politics of strife. In fact, I believed that my creative talents were better placed in entertainment and the arts than in solely marching and direct action. The arts could be harnessed to tell a story and embrace a political message.

I had left a strong ents team in my wake and knew that my successors would continue the high level of ents promotion I had been lucky enough to establish. But what career would make sense for me after these wild Bristol days?

My first move was a short but frustrating stint as a grounds' maintenance staffer for Bristol City Council, where I was responsible for painting white lines on a football field. I would walk the length of each field pushing a device that bled white lime to mark the outer edges of the playing field. I also needed to mark out the goal post area including the important penalty spot. It was here that I decided I could test my creativity and exercise my rebellious nature. Instead of dropping a single blob of lime to mark the penalty spot, I built up, layer by layer, a white mound some inches high, with the fanciful notion that the penalty kicker would not only kick the ball into the goal but in doing so would create an explosion of white lime powder as the kicker's foot met the mound, so adding some theatrical excitement to the game. Frustratingly, I was never able to witness whether this spectacular moment occurred, but I suspected the chief groundsman would launch an investigation. It was time to make my escape!

Finding the Arts

1979 was the year Margaret Thatcher assumed office as prime minister of Britain. Her political vision was to loosen the bureaucratic strings of government, reduce local authority spending, reduce the power of the trade unions, and create an enterprising Britain out of a socialist Britain. My lowly position in the local authority was unaffected at the time but the word "cuts" began to take on an ominous meaning for me.

Bristol had taught me that the entertainments business was needed, whether in war or in peace, and so I determined that if I received some formal training in entertainments, I would be able to develop a career in the business. I saw an ad for a trainee arts and entertainment position in Hemel Hempstead, a so-called new town designed to house families that had been displaced from the London Blitz. The town's most notable feature was its Magic Roundabout. The distinctive feature of the roundabout was that it allowed traffic to flow both clockwise and anti-clockwise, in some town planner's dream design. I now live in the US where roundabouts seem to terrify and confuse the average American driver, so the thought of one that moves in either direction would be their worst nightmare!

The trainee position that I had applied for was to work for the town's local government entertainment division, part of Dacorum District Council. In Bristol, I had been the king of entertainments – in Hemel Hempstead, I was a mere junior. After leaving Bristol, I had considered pursuing a career in the music business. However, after working in the business first-hand, I realised the fickle nature of a career in pop music management. So, I thought at least working for a local authority would provide some stability.

My duties involved front-of-house management for many diverse types of public events, from rock concerts to televised wrestling, boxing matches to ballroom dancing. I also helped in the main concert hall's box office, selling tickets. I was responsible for balancing cash and making banking arrangements at the end of the day. I completed two years' experience in these entertainment management functions, and while I recognized the need to attend to and learn these functions within the context of a local authority department, I found most of this work extremely dull and tedious.

So, to help me to find a way of progressing from these types of duties, during this period I took a correspondence course leading to a diploma in entertainments industry management. The course was sponsored by The Institute of Municipal Entertainments. The course covered topics in event management, publicity, production and distribution, safety, legal and policy issues. Once I had qualified, I was put in charge of running Hemel Hempstead's annual carnival. This involved liaising with the local police and community organisations in coordinating preparations for the town parade and the carnival fair events. The scale and nature of this carnival in fact did little to excite me, although I would later be able to compare this tame provincial event with a rather better-known international carnival event...

I was no fan of working for any authority, let alone a local town authority. My trainee role meant that I would often be shadowing a very drunken staff member as he slurred through his day, booking boxing matches and the occasional rock concert. Max's (not his real name) day largely ended a little after 11 am when he sloped off to the pub for a gin lunch. He would return, sometime after 3 pm, to put in, ooh, another 20 minutes of work time before heading home. The joys of wasteful council employment in the early eighties!

During my two-year period with Dacorum council, I was transferred to the local arts centre to help manage their programme of events. The council had redeveloped the old town hall to create what became titled the Old Town Hall Arts Centre. It had been refurbished with a stage, a seating system, theatre lighting, stage electrics and catering facilities. A director had been appointed to plan and manage its arts events. This arts centre held much more interest for me than the town's large, modern multipurpose entertainments hall.

The director, Robert Adams, a former British Petroleum employee who had been responsible for BP's sponsorship of the prestigious Egon Ronay restaurant guide, turned out to be one of the most inventive arts programmers I have ever come across. Not being content with merely promoting amateur theatre groups, he served up an eclectic diet of international mime performances, puppetry and even a series of cooking shows by top London restaurant chefs. These master cooks would prepare first-class gourmet meals in front of a paying audience. Of course, this style of entertainment is now popular on TV but back then, in the early 80s in a theatre setting it was unusual and innovative, and proved to be extremely popular.

My duties at the arts centre were to stage-manage events and help incoming theatre groups set up props and lights. During my time at the centre, I met a fascinating variety of performers, cooks, puppeteers and mime artists. I was also sent on a trainee course in Bell and Howell projectors so I could show films at the refurbished Old Town Hall Arts Centre.

Robert had exquisite taste in all things and brought a sense of finery to the arts that was absent for me in country fairs and boxing matches, the staples of the town's main entertainments division. I was lucky enough to be his right-hand assistant and I loved the work!

One day, the fine arts were disturbed by a dawn culling of pigeons. Pigeon poop was apparently causing some distress to pavement walkers who would slip on freshly dispensed white faeces. The dawn cull, with the chosen method involving shooting the pigeons, was not without controversy and was quite a bloody affair. When I arrived at work that morning pigeon blood was spattered everywhere, on the Town Hall steps and on the pavement. The pigeons were gone, deceased, but the controversy of shooting vs poisoning or simply letting the pigeons do as they pleased stayed with the Arts Centre for some months. On reflection this might have inspired a Tom Lehrer musical, *Poisoning Pigeons for the Arts*, and thus helped at the centre box office.

The Arts and Entertainments Manager for the council, Mick Jones, had some theatre directing experience and had used this, and his position and knowledge of theatre, to assemble a professional touring theatre company for the council. I was given responsibility for booking and stage-managing the company in community venues in the locality. It was during this period I learned about touring theatre, including all the exhilaration it could bring, and the pitfalls.

Mick Jones also arranged an internship for me at a community arts enterprise in London. I was interviewed by Ed Berman, the founder and director of InterAction, and was placed in the theatre department. It was to be one of the most valuable professional experiences of my life.

London Land

As much as I loved working in the arts in Hemel Hempstead, this was not exactly an arts mecca, whereas London, not far down the road, of course was, so I was determined to find employment there in the arts. I found that position working for InterAction, a multi-mission arts and educational foundation.

The founder, US-born Ed Berman, held dual citizenship in the US and the UK. He developed his extraordinary vision of providing innovative activities for urban communities as a way of, if not improving the lives of local people, then at least temporarily diverting their attention from the pressing problems of the inner city. Ed's emphasis was on innovation, education and training, and the use and promotion of anything new, anything offbeat, outrageous, or just different. Ed had an outstanding ability to raise money for these multifarious enterprises. In 1982, inner-city advisor to Margaret Thatcher, Michael Heseltine, appointed Ed to advise him on how to tackle the many issues facing the UK's inner cities. Heseltine asked Ed for a one-pager of ideas. In typical Ed style, he took the notion of a one-pager as preliminary guidance only and, using the creative assets of InterAction, created a floor-sized one-pager packed with ideas on engaging inner-city youth away from the riots that were endemic in Britain at the time. Ed was awarded an MBE for his work in the inner cities.

InterAction was an extraordinary enterprise. To say it was a group of multimedia enterprises would not do sufficient justice to the breadth of its work. InterAction had theatre units, audio and visual studios, a publishing arm, a graphics studio, a school, a city farm, and an international division. It was a not-for-profit enterprise funded by the local council, charitable foundations, and corporations. The company also derived income from the sales of books, theatre shows, training courses, and bar and catering sales. Ed's philosophy was one of social enterprise, a sort of melding of the enterprising spirit of capitalism with the caring elements of socialism.

InterAction, with its wide range of facilities – production, video, audio, design, printing, photography, rehearsal room, farm, school, etc. – was well-equipped to bring all this off. It had no religious or political affiliation, yet people who worked there were called either members or associates. Wages were assessed on needs, not skills. Members were required to live in InterAction group housing that was supplied with food and household provisions. However, I wasn't attracted to this live-in lifestyle, and so I managed to opt out of living in their group housing.

Having learned the basics in my ents role, I was now able to learn so much more from Ed about publicity, event management, fundraising and implementing big ideas. I also undertook a variety of one- and two-week training courses in the use of video, photography, and sound equipment in community arts activities. These courses also encompassed theatre management, oral history projects, memory, direct mail, fundraising and public speaking. I also learned valuable marketing and publicity skills while attending a marketing seminar organized by Eastern Arts, a UK regional arts council. During this period, I also joined the Society of London Arts Publicists and the National Association of Arts Centres (UK) and was exposed to the then current theories and practices in arts publicity and management.

My job at InterAction was to manage the theatre activities of the various company theatre units. The 'Almost Free Theatre' was a fringe (in New York parlance, an off-off-Broadway) touring company that toured productions by new playwrights. 'Professor Doggs Troupe' was the educational theatre company that had an extensive summer touring programme as well as mounting school shows and cameo performances. My job was to book all the tours, arrange publicity, write and distribute press releases, arrange photo shoots, collate performance statistics for funders, maintain prop inventories and undertake all the other associated administrative matters concerned with the running of active touring theatre units.

Because of this, my attentions were focused on the educational theatre units under the Prof Doggs Troupe banner. Now, these were innovative companies, so much so that they bucked the folkloric trend of not mixing actors and animals, and developed an educational show using actors interacting with goats, sheep, and snakes (yes, really!). Not only did I have to arrange bed and breakfast accommodation for the actors on tour, but I also joked that I was the only theatre booker who had to arrange bed and breakfast for two sheep, a goat and an anaconda snake!

One Prof. Doggs Troupe theatre unit was known as the 'Animobile'. The Animobile show had human characters, plus two sheep and a goat, props, all in aid of a silly plot that was designed to teach young people where milk comes from, how butter is made, the origin of woollen garments and other educational topics. The anaconda snake made special guest appearances. The 'Radio Van', meanwhile, was a specially converted Mercedes van that housed video and audio equipment. This was used to create the *Radio Van Show*, which had characters, props and a plot designed to teach kids how to make radio and video programmes. The kids had total control over each programme's content. The actors and technical staff traveling with the Radio Van were there to help draw ideas out of the kids. Each radio show developed by the kids was passed on to BBC Radio London for local broadcast.

Local city and town authorities booked these touring theatre units for their summer entertainments programmes in parks and recreation areas. Some authorities would book the units for a week, others for a day or an afternoon. The summer months were busiest, as I would have four touring units out on the road at any one time. During the rest of the year, I booked a programme called 'Dolls Shows'. Dolls Shows used half-size puppets in performances for kindergarten age children. The shows were highly acclaimed by education advisors.

I promoted these touring programmes using a variety of techniques. I maintained (pre-computers!) card index lists of regular bookers and used these to send out direct mail pieces to prospective organisations. I also ran a crude but effective telemarketing programme. The facilities of InterAction were such that mounting a trade show exhibition for would-be local authority bookers was easily accomplished. Using the design, photography, and video staff, I mounted two trade shows at local authority entertainment conventions.

One interesting programme, Ed, as artistic director of InterAction, had developed was cameo productions where professional actors would take on the mantle of historical characters. The twist was that the actors never broke character, nor did they operate on a stage. Two cameo productions the company developed were of Captain Cook, the explorer, and William Shakespeare.

Each actor spent about nine months developing his character and researching the life history of his chosen persona. It was an intense process that culminated in the public 'coming out' of each character. I recall one fascinating evening where we took both Shakespeare and Captain Cook out to the pub to converse with locals. The idea was that it would help them build the actors' confidence

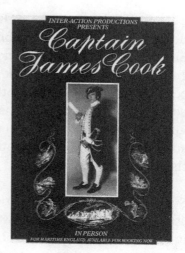

Captain Cook cameo brochure for Maritime England campaign

in their characters before being invited before a paying public gathering.

This was 1982 and the Argentineans had just invaded the Falkland Islands. The British had responded by sending a naval flotilla to the South Atlantic. The pub was therefore buzzing with Malvinas and Falkland Islands topics and hot-headed political discussion. At 8:30pm on that weekday night in Kentish Town, London, in walked Captain James Cook and William Shakespeare in full regalia, talking in the language common to their respective historical periods.

Among the customers, in the pub that night was the film actor Bob Hoskins. The stage was set for a lively evening. Both Cook and Shakespeare engaged the locals in a fascinating discourse of comparative battle stories and social history through the ages, as former and present-day war preparations and political attitudes were argued and discussed. Bob Hoskins, who was local to the area, appeared highly amused and unfazed by this unusual gathering.

Captain Cook received sponsorship from the English Tourist Board, helping them to promote tourism events throughout England. When they were not under contract to the English Tourist Board, I booked Cook and Shakespeare into schools and community organisations. Both Cook and Shakespeare attracted contracts in the United States and the Northern Territories of Australia. While I didn't travel with the performers, I handled the administrative bookings, contracts and travel arrangements for these overseas cameo tours.

Such was the stuff of InterAction theatre productions. One other strange but inventive show was a production called *Show Trial*. It was Ed's idea to stage a mock trial of the Arts Council of Great Britain. We staged the event at the Tricycle Theatre in Kilburn in Northwest London. The idea was to use real artists who would present their trial evidence in their chosen arts form, whatever form their art took.

The production had a core group of actors playing judge, prosecution and defence, and a loose script that allowed for different artists to present their artistic evidence in the form of new (and rather wild) sound poetry, sculpture, painting, comedy, and straight theatrical performance. Each show night was different and required extensive talent scouting for performers and artists. This was improvisational theatre at its finest.

The charge against the Arts Council was that it was failing to uphold the duties enacted in its founding charter, which were to preserve, foster and promote the arts in Britain.

I stayed at InterAction for two years. I had amassed valuable skills, ones that I could replicate later in life in so many other professional endeavours. At 28, I decided I needed a new challenge, something I could look back on and feel I had achieved something. I accepted the job of raising some £2 million ($3.5 million) to build a new theatre in the East End of London.

The Half Moon Theatre

So, in 1983, now 28 years old, I moved from InterAction to the Half Moon Theatre, having been attracted to the idea of helping to build a new theatre in the East End of London. The existing theatre was known for its musicals, West End transfers and politically left productions. In return for a salary of £7,500 per year my job was fundraising to build a new theatre on land behind the present theatre, which was housed in an old Wesleyan chapel. This fundraising exercise helped me to define sharply our goals and break down challenges into manageable portions. It had to be this way, as the odds against raising the £2 million we needed, in one chunk, were overwhelming.

That part of London, east of Tower Bridge and near the docks, is known for its grittiness and its chipper and hardworking cockney soul. It's an area where the smell of vinegar-racked seafood stalls mingles with the smell of beer brewing. It's the area where in 1888 serial killer Jack the Ripper mutilated and killed female prostitutes. Now, 100 years later, our most famous resident was another Jack, Jack Dash, a British communist and trade union leader, famous for his role in the London dock strike. Jack used to mingle among the theatre patrons as they queued for each night's show, as he enjoyed the banter and fresh seafood outside the theatre chapel.

The East End also had a long theatrical tradition and was known for its many houses of entertainment in the Victorian era and early twentieth century. Parts of the area had decayed when London had lost its importance as a shipping and dockside area. In 1983 it was then under extensive redevelopment as part of an enterprise zone promoted by the Conservative government. It was here, in these colourful and gritty urban surroundings, I now felt lay the opportunity for me to make a mark.

This period in my life became more than just a challenge – it was my political and societal maturation. Britain at the time, under its prime minister Margaret Thatcher, was an intensely political era. You had to be either right- or left-wing inclined. There was no in-between. You were for or against the privatisation of nationalised industries. Being pro the miners' strike meant more than just an attitude – you had to be involved. You had to raise money, wear a badge, attend a meeting, or house a striking miner in your home when the miners were campaigning and touring the country.

I had assumed, early on in my new position, that I could raise funds through soliciting collections after shows, sponsorships of parts of the building, and community activities. It was later that I realised the naivety of generating funds merely from paper collections and brick sponsorships. The real funding potential lay in securing a major political investment by a local authority. Clearly, most funding would have to come from the Greater London Council (GLC), the regional elected authority for the capital, and from the borough of Tower Hamlets, the local council for that part of London. The problem was that Margaret Thatcher was intent on abolishing the GLC. London would be left as the only major western capital city without an elected authority.

The GLC was very pro arts funding, but the competition for funds was fierce. You had to make a convincing case. Tony Banks was the Chair of the Arts and Recreation Committee, and while he was supportive, he had to attend to a crowded and competitive field of other arts organisations that were each putting forward a worthy cause. The authority had a team of funding specialists that would examine funding proposals very carefully before they disbursed funds. The chairman of our appeal committee was Illtyd Harrington, deputy leader of the GLC. That connection helped enormously, and we secured two or three large grants totalling £300,000 or so from the GLC before its demise. I attended all the council committee meetings and had extensive discussions with council officers during this period.

While the Appeal Committee meeting was chaired by Illtyd Harrington, I also co-opted a local developer and adviser to the London Docklands Development. When I later raised funds from trade unions, I knew I was walking a fundraising tightrope by bringing together corporate business with trade union leaders. I also knew that the theatre had a good reputation in theatrical and local circles, so I continued to woo the development community.

In tandem with these two fundraising strategies, I set up a system to raise funds from charitable foundations. I hired a freelance fundraiser. His job was to establish a direct mail operation to send funding proposals to all foundations and trusts that had an interest in either the East End of London, theatre, or young people. Foundations and charitable trusts, by their nature, are secretive species. I was uncertain about the results we might achieve through this strategy. The occasional cheque for £2,000, £5,000, and even £10,000 did arrive, but they made only partial dents in the massive monetary target we had to meet. One such cheque came from Robert Maxwell, newspaper proprietor and owner of the Daily Mirror, a Labour-supporting paper. Maxwell had sent one of his staff with a £5,000 or £10,000 cheque. At the time, the Half Moon theatre offices consisted of a converted single-decker red London bus. This was certainly a memorable and distinctive office, in line with the type of theatre we were trying to create! One day I noticed the man looking around the bus. I asked him in, and he handed me a cheque and wished us well. Whether it was that cheque or another that made the difference, we were able to upgrade the offices to a bright red double-decker bus.

L-R Ray Buckton General Secretary ASLEF & Author outside the Half Moon Theatre chapel

Using the funds we raised, the publicity manager, Nick, was also able to upgrade the theatre's computer facilities to help manage press releases and publicity materials. Nick called me to his desk and excitedly said that his new machine could spellcheck what he wrote! Nick Starr went on to become a very successful general manager of the National Theatre.

Another source of funds was urban development grants. These were grants made available by the Department of the

Environment to help urban area renewal. The competition for this type of funding was intense, as all the local community and arts organisations put in bids. This element of funding required a cautious series of local meetings to gauge the political support or antagonism toward the theatre. I had been working closely with the theatre's architect, Florian Beigel, and the building team, throughout the development phase. Through Florian, I formed an appreciation of architecture as well as learning about theatre construction. I enlisted the services of the development team to help with fundraising presentations.

I was aware then that the trade union movement in Britain had designs on securing a home for a labour movement theatre in the UK. I therefore established a separate strategy to raise funds from the trade unions. I invited the leaders of the railway and transportation unions to the theatre for discussions and theatre performances. I also arranged a presentation and exhibition about the theatre at a trade union council meeting in a central London hotel. As a result of these trade union meetings and strategies, I was able to secure moderate trade union investment totalling about £20,000. I was still a considerable way off the final goal. We needed a broader political strategy.

The National Campaign for the Arts arose out of a meeting of arts and theatre groups at the Old Vic theatre in London. Arts practitioners realised that the only way to counter government policies in the arts was to combine forces. This meant that arts managers had to sit down with arts unions. Theatre people had to talk to music people. Modern art painters had to sit

NATIONAL CAMPAIGN FOR THE
ARTS

FOUNDING MEMBERS

Stephen Remington, Charlotte Ashe, Pierre Audi, Joan Bakewell, David Brierley, Peter Brinson, Peter Conway, Carol Crowe, Les Cullen, Peter Finch, John Fox, G. Laurence Harbottle, Robin Howard, Remi Kapo, Carol Kenna, Errol Lloyd, John Morton, Steve Murphy, Nicholas Payne, Peter Plouviez, David Richardson, Jack Stoddart, Bob Swash, David Aukin, Peter Stark, Olivia Maxwell, Michael Attenborough, Jude Kelly, Michael Bogdanov, Claire Venables, Mamoun Hasaan, John Crisp, Ian Ritchie, Ian Robertson, Clive Smart.

National Campaign for the Arts

at the same table as museum curators. This was the eventual outcome of the National Campaign for the Arts, a broad-based organisation concerned with the preservation and promotion of the arts in Britain.

British Actors' Equity, The Musicians' Union, The British Orchestras' Association, museum curators and artists representative groups all helped to form this organisation, raised funds, wrote a constitution, hired staff, rented an office, and produced publicity and campaign resource materials. It was a period I value greatly in so many ways. I had the opportunity to work with a diverse and top-level group of people like the general secretary of Equity, Peter Plouviez, and John Morton, General Secretary of the Musicians' Union.

It was during this period I realised the value of sound research and effective copywriting. Through our research, we discovered that cheese received more public subsidies in Britain than the arts. I tried to verify this piece of trivia with the Department of Agriculture, realising it would make a powerful campaign copy. However, my research did teach me a lot about cheese and the complexity of European cheese subsidies! The subsidies were so complex that it proved to be difficult to verify the statement.

I was on the founding committee of the National Campaign for the Arts for one year before the organisation opened nominations for election. The campaign and what was happening in London and the arts spurred my need to play a role in defending the arts. *To Cap It All* was our, as arts practitioners, way of campaigning against policies

To Cap It All - Rate Capping concert

which were threatening the arts while providing a diverse entertainment for Londoners. We held this event at the Royal Festival Hall and enlisted David Blunkett MP to help spread the word to his political network.

We booked and staged acts from jugglers to socialist magicians, a 50s doo-wop group, stand-up comedy, and rock and roll bands. Emma Thompson agreed to perform alongside Jim Carter, Sylvia Sims, Adrian Henri, Arthur Mullard, Maureen Lipman, and Darts. I scoured the stage shops in London's West End theatre section for bowler hats. The idea was to throw these hats out to the crowd at

Daily Telegraph review Sept 18, 1984

the end of the evening to promote the image of a privileged and bowler-hatted upper class handing out funding cuts to ordinary Londoners.

We promoted *To Cap It All* by distributing posters on hoardings all over London. We also arranged a photo call with the Leader of the Greater London Council, Ken Livingstone, and some of the cabaret entertainers. The event was so successful that even the naturally conservative Daily Telegraph gave it a good review. Thirty-five years later, I discovered a copy of the *To Cap It All* concert programme on eBay and promptly bought it. The seller told me her parents had taken her for a walk along the South Bank in London and they saw the concert poster and decided to attend, hence the programme!

The Half Moon played an important role in bringing theatre to the East End of London, but we faced competition from the better-funded Shakespeare Globe Theatre, whose fundraising was led by American actor Sam Wanamaker. My fundraising was no match for that of the Globe Theatre, even with the modest financial input from the development and the trade union community. Still, we did open the theatre on April 29th 1985, with Chris Bond's magnificent production of *Sweeney Todd*. So many well-known actors have cut their acting chops at the Half Moon, including Daniel Day-Lewis, who played Dracula in Chris Bond's 1984 production. A cappella group the Mint Juleps, formed from front-of-house staff, became mainstays at the theatre before being signed to Stiff Records. They were later hired as musical entertainment for Virgin's inaugural flight to the US.

America in Sight

My brother, Bernard, had at this time accepted a job in Florida in the United States. Whether in the US or in England, Florida was well-known as an exotic holiday destination. So, I insisted on visiting Bernard at the earliest opportunity. That opportunity arose in 1981. My exposure to American culture had been limited to cowboy and detective films. As a Brit, America was the promised land.

The vision of landing in Miami is still etched in my mind. The lights and geographical symmetry of the city were such a novel experience for me. The easy exotic lifestyle was a complete change from the colder, slower, harder, urban UK lifestyle back home. I relished the beaches, the blondness, and the food. But after a week, I quickly tired of it all.

So, I caught a Greyhound bus to California. The journey took three days. I remember being awed by the sights of New Orleans, Bourbon Street, and the Saguaro cactus of New Mexico.

After having been so recently in the United States and exposed to the full force of capitalism, I swallowed hard on my return to England and the Half Moon Theatre and hired a staff member to raise funds from the corporate sector. I say swallowed hard because pitting the trade unions and corporate sector in a joint venture was a tricky prospect in the political atmosphere that existed in Britain at this time. I hired a co-worker who had been working in an organisation designed to help arts organisations raise funds from the corporate sector.

My fundraising colleague invited Lord Gowrie, the Arts Minister of the day, to a reception at the theatre. Lord Gowrie, a Conservative, was very pro-business funding for the arts and could offer welcome political as well as business support.

In April 1986, we opened stage one of the theatre to the public. We had at this point raised over one million pounds, and to me this felt like a moment of great achievement. Unfortunately, though, the Half Moon was not producing revenue of the sort it needed to justify its Arts Council and local authority funding. Things unravelled fast. The management of the theatre fell quickly into disarray, to the point that members of staff staged a coup one day to force out the theatre's general manager. Matters just got even worse at that point. The Artistic Director, Chris Bond, who had been directing *Sweeney Todd* in Sweden, hurried back from there to attempt to sort out the theatre's gross debt and absence of management. And then, a bombshell was dropped. Almost half the staff were laid off, me included. I received redundancy pay of £750. The building development was put on hold, and the theatre went dark. I had learnt so much and had put my heart and soul into the ambitious £2 million fundraising push for the Half Moon, but its name was now horribly apposite – we had reached half that sum, but this proved to just not be enough to save it at that point. I was 31 years old.

I decided to escape Britain and travelled to Barcelona, Spain, to visit my younger brother, Sean, who had been living there for about two years. My newfound love of architecture led me to an appreciation of the work of the Spanish architect, Gaudi, whose buildings and amazing cathedral are some of the greatest landmarks in Barcelona. We rented a car and travelled down the coast through Valencia and Alicante to Grenada and the Moorish-built Alhambra fort. This trip gave me the chance to breathe again and experience many of the Easter pageants and festivities that are endemic in the cities and towns of Spain.

Labour London

When I returned from Spain, through friends, I found a job at a Labour Movement-based public relations firm called LMS, for Labour Movement Services. LMS focussed on supporting labour and trade union organisations and combined political with cultural events. I admired the LMS owners for their commitment to the cause, though often wondered if their world music events and cassette tape sales, and their historic recreations of marches, made any money. Having altruistic beliefs and generating an income was hard to do then and remains so!

One of the events I was tasked with managing was the London concert debut of Panamanian singer, Ruben Blades. A much-admired musician and actor in Panama and throughout Latin America, Blades had the ambition to be a leader of Panama. At the time, I had not heard of him, which proved to be a distinct disadvantage for someone responsible for his UK debut.

I made flight arrangements for Ruben Blades and his entourage to schedule them into Britain from their European leg of the group's tour. I also arranged hotel accommodation and limousine transportation for the group during their stay. I then organized a press conference to announce the star's arrival and upcoming concert dates. I booked a London hotel room to accommodate the music and arts media and Ruben for the press event. I was astonished that the press conference attracted so much attention. I was embarrassed to end up having reporters queuing to get in the room.

My experience in music promotion was enormously helpful in helping me to remember to cover all the bases required in show promotion. I arranged poster distribution, drinks, and food for the backstage crew, and liaised over audio and lighting hire with our production staff. The concert sold well, and my fears about the popularity of salsa music in Britain were assuaged.

After the Ruben Blades concert, I was given another music role at LMS, to promote a world music festival for Haringey Council. The festival gave me the opportunity to retrace my music agency roots. As the local council was the festival sponsor, I also met with the political leadership office of Bernie Grant to discuss the arrangements for the event. My knowledge of

Haringey Festival Against Racism

public administration and policy was helpful in being able to help the council realise its goals. I contracted a line-up of reggae, salsa and soul performers, including Dennis Brown, Ruby Turner, Ray Barretto and Eddie Palmieri. The festival was a great success, with its diverse and interesting range of music attracting about 10,000 people.

My final project for LMS was to promote the 50th anniversary of the Jarrow March. This Jarrow March event had been dreamt up by two enterprising young men from Leeds, England, Richard Haswell and Simon Osborn. They had come up with the idea of recreating the famous Jarrow unemployment march of 1936 as a 50th-anniversary event. Present-day unemployed people from

Mr Claude Robinson one of the original Jarrow marchers, with organisers Simon Osborn left and Richard Haswell right while Liz Brailsford holds the petition box. Alan Hull from the pop group Lindisfarne is pictured to the right of Claude.

the north of England took the place of the 1936 marchers. This was a period of particularly high unemployment, with many feeling similar levels of despair as those who had been moved to march 50 years previously. Therefore, the goal of the march was to promote the plight of the unemployed in Britain and to raise the level of debate about the government's economic policies. Alongside the march there was to be a travelling theatre show and a commemorative record album. It was a hugely ambitious undertaking, but the founders had the event well organized and had received funding from trade unions. Lindisfarne band leader and brilliant songwriter Alan Hull joined us on the tour, providing musical accompaniment along the way. The Jarrow venture met my ambition to use cultural initiatives to address political issues.

My job was to attract national and local media attention along the route of the march. I set up a media database using the database technology of the time, a very simple flat file database called 'Cardbox'. While not as sophisticated as the database technology available today, it was a step up from the card index system I had been using in InterAction. I entered the names and contact information for all the national and regional media in the UK as well as entering international media organisations like Reuters and other wire services. I planned releases to go out as the tour progressed along the 300-mile route from North Shields to London. I also arranged a photoshoot some months before the start of the march in the British press's so-called 'silly season', the summer months. We tracked down an original 1930s marcher for the photocall.

The Jarrow March provided me with the opportunity to exercise all my media management skills. I arranged a press launch at the start of the march and carried a cellular phone to call en route and schedule information to local media as we entered towns along the march route.

While there were a variety of political opinions amongst the organisers and marchers, I felt that to attract sympathetic coverage, we should present a non-political and human side to the Jarrow marchers' story. I therefore arranged careful briefings with marchers I selected to go on camera or provide interviews to the print press.

It was a hectic schedule to coordinate local, regional and national press coverage along the route. At one point, the BBC arranged to fly me and two marchers from northern England to London for a lunchtime TV talk show, then fly us back to re-join the march. In Leeds, we arranged for the unemployed marchers to speak during a live outside broadcast on a TV breakfast show.

When I was in London, before the start of the march, I had arranged for a media monitoring service to fax TV and radio transcripts to the agency office. I also arranged for a newspaper clipping service to send press clips. Two memorable photo shoots were with the Labour Party leader, Neil Kinnock, along the route of the march and outside the houses of parliament. Another memorable photo shot was a recreation of a famous picture taken in 1936 at the midpoint of the march. The recreated photo showed a 'then and now' picture of the marchers. We designed it to have a pictorial impact to show that not much had changed in economic and employment policies in fifty years. The event ended in London with a political rally in Trafalgar Square. During the same period, I arranged press coverage for the travelling theatre show and the record album launch that we cross-promoted with the march.

So impressed were the Labour Party at the extent of the Jarrow marchers' level of national and international press on the topic of unemployment that they invited us down to Labour Party headquarters. I sat opposite Neil Kinnock's newly appointed Director of Communications, Peter Mandelson, as he asked me why we had attracted so much publicity at a time when the Labour Party was struggling to gain attention for the issue of youth unemployment. There were several reasons for our publicity successes. First, we humanised the story by offering disadvantaged unemployed youth the opportunity to tell their unadulterated story on camera. This was not a policy story about unemployment but a cultural event with real people. Second, we focused on local news by calling the media as we entered each town. I had assembled a list of media in each locality and called the local press on a brick-sized mobile phone. The media dutifully showed up as our march support bus, theatre and musical entourage and young marchers offered a prize media spectacle as we entered each town. The story itself, a recreation of a famous march, complete with 1930 vs 1980s juxtaposed photos, was made for visual media both on television and in print. I had hoped that our humanisation of the tragedy of youth unemployment, with a tightly organised press relations operation, might not only raise national attention but that our approach might inform Labour Party HQ that politics can in fact be fun. I was endeavouring to show that they could gain human and emotional appeal and need not always be just putting out the strident policy-based appeals that in the mid-1980s seemed to be doing little to advance the Labour Party cause.

CHAPTER 4:
A GREAT ESCAPE

The Sizzle of Self

After Jarrow, I needed a break and found it in the Greek Islands. It took a moonlit stroll near the port town of Paros to learn there was more to Greece than heat, and more in me than an English Catholic boys boarding school schooling had allowed me to reveal. I was 27 when I had first visited a hot country. Born in England, my family had spent summers in Ireland and the Isle of Man, both ferry rides across the Irish Sea. Ireland is famous for having more than the usual six types of rain known to northerners – very light rain, light rain, moderate rain, heavy rain, very heavy rain, and extreme rain. Our family summers were a chance to experience 17 different types of rain, including drizzle, sideways drizzle, mist, exceptionally cold mist, spitting rain, driving rain, freezing rain, hail, and annoyingly rain that first goes sideways then underneath your collar. The Isle of Man added fog to this list, and the weather was always the subject of an abject apology from my uncle, ashamed of his homeland for affording us such a rotten holiday. If the temperature reached 68 degrees the newspaper headlines would screech, "Phew Wotta Scorcher!" But summers in Britain were always like this. It seemed

I was alone among my friends in not fleeing English summers for Greece, that is until I reached an age when I could afford it.

The ferry from Piraeus, the mainland port, to Paros takes four hours, four hours to drench yourself in sun on the top deck and dream about which of the dozens of European young female travellers could possibly have any interest in me. My friends said that Paros was the place where it was almost impossible not to get laid. The warm ambience, the stark nakedness of everyone on the beach, combined with ouzo, retsina, cheap Greek beer, Euro discos and simply the energy of a few hundred twenty-something souls was surely a sure-fire recipe for more than idle tourism. Turned out, for everyone except me. I laid in wait for the special moment I felt sure would come, staying late at the table after a restaurant dinner, hanging out at the beach cafe at night, waiting for my fantasy to come true. I first went to Greece in 1985 and returned to England having waited in vain. I felt cheated, well-tanned, but cheated from the carnal fantasy I had been led to believe was not only in my grasp but so abundant, like Greek bouzouki music – an irritating grating sound I never got a taste for. And so, I conjured the thought that my friends had been false prophets.

Still, I ventured to Paros for a second summer the following year, in the hope that sand and sizzle would not end as a fizzle in my newly-discovered land. And so, I ambled down the cobbled streets of Logaras, Paros, after spending another sun-soaked day on the beach lying among dozens of naked young people, nervous that a sudden female attraction would not cause a noticeable stirring reaction in my prone, well-oiled but vulnerable body. But that was the thing with nakedness – it all seemed so routine after a while. At night when we retired to a restaurant, the oft-heard words were, "Oh, I didn't recognize you with your clothes on."

But there was something about Greece and the air that night that caused a shift in me. I had had a conversation earlier that day on the beach with Sharon, a friend's girlfriend who I was smitten with. She said that here on the island, "You wear your heart on your sleeve." My vulnerable self shone through, and she knew from my eyes I was seriously attracted to her. She opened a path to susceptibility in me. As I walked to the restaurant that evening, I was hypnotised by the medicinal smell of the eucalyptus trees that lined the narrow streets. I gazed over the bay and saw the moon reflecting white on the Mediterranean Sea. I searched for a reference from my past, a way to capture this point in time, to freeze frame, to suck it in, to seduce me. I exclaimed to my friends that I wished I could inhale the scene, to smoke it like a drug and feel it penetrate my pores. They laughed, saying only I could have made a reference like that.

After dinner we went to the beach cafe for drinks. A couple of people had guitars and played popular songs from the 70s and 80s. I asked to borrow a harmonica and found harmony with the melodies. A young blond woman joined us. We all sang and drank late, playing rhythms as the warm night Med wind blew across the moonlit shore. The eucalyptic freshness, the heady drinks, the music, and the touch of the woman's smooth blond hair, the freeness of the night opened a doorway in me. As the night folded into morning, we walked along the sand until we found an open view of the sea. We lay down, took off our few remaining clothes. I savoured her before entering and sensing her essence I laid her out before me and softly touched her rippled surface then slowly unfolded, squeezed, pierced, and juiced her sweet skin. I had an early morning ferry back to Piraeus so left her sensual and naked body asleep on the beach to return to London life.

My temporary position at the public relations agency had finished in late November of 1986. I spent the remainder of November and early December travelling. I revisited my brother in Barcelona. I then travelled on to Amsterdam where I stayed on a houseboat close to the famous red-light district of the city. I was away from

England for about two or three weeks and dreaded the thought of returning to no job.

When I returned, I was fortunate to receive a call from a colleague I had worked with at InterAction, Bob Chase. He was then working for a local authority just north of London as an arts and entertainments officer. He asked me if I would book the council's season of summer activities for children. He knew I had the experience of contracting artists and arranging this kind of programme. I was employed as a freelancer on contract. I enjoyed researching events and activities for children again, and eventually put together a programme of inflatables, theatre, clowns and workshops lasting four weeks. I was thankful though that my job was just to contract these events. I did not have to stay to manage them. My contract with the authority ended when I presented them with the events schedule and performance contracts.

By February of 1987, and at 32, I felt England had served its usefulness to me. Life on the dole between contract work was depressing. I had a girlfriend from my Bristol student days, Susan, who had been traveling in the Caribbean and South America for about nine months and was still travelling in South America. I was receiving regular letters and postcards from Ecuador, Peru, Chile and other exotic places. She had suggested I visit her, and so one weekend I mentally prepared myself to fly out and meet her in Rio de Janeiro, Brazil. The plan was to spend six weeks in Rio and then return to England to continue my search for a job. I packed a bag containing shorts, two t-shirts, toiletries, a Bible, a set of harmonicas, and curiously, my CV.

Cidade Maravilhosa!

I t's healthy to bare one's soul and one's buttocks in Rio. One might say of Brazil that in Rio, buttocks and soul are one. The torsos on Copacabana beach, the carnival, and the rhythm of the language, fluid, like a verbal lambada dance, lie as a testament to this theory. I had arrived from a country known for its stuffiness and prudishness to one where emotions and bodies are brazenly displayed.

Before leaving England, I had picked up a Portuguese phrase book, after first making the typical mistake of believing Brazilians spoke Spanish. I also picked up a guide to Rio and a notebook to write in. I needed injections for yellow fever and hepatitis before I left. Although this was the height of the AIDS crisis, in Brazil, dengue fever seemed to garner more attention than AIDS. The plane arrived in Rio on February 27, 1987. Susan met me at the airport, and we travelled by city bus together to her hotel, Turistico Hotel, a short walk from the Gloria metro station and a short walk to the city centre.

It was the start of carnival season. I went to Rio Branco, the main city thoroughfare, in the evening for the start of carnival proper. Transvestites abounded in large numbers, gaily prancing through the crowds. I found myself thinking that it was difficult to distinguish the sex of people in the crowds.

We bought tickets for the main samba parade in the Sambadrome, a specially designed stadium street with tiered seating. We arrived at 6pm complete with sandwiches of avocado and garlic, lots of caipirinha, the local very strong sugar cane drink. One man inflated a condom and started to pass it along the crowd. Another local started a chant about imprisoned South African leader, Nelson Mandela. The ubiquitous sellers selling peanuts, drink, beer and coffee all had their individual ways of capturing your attention amongst the spectacle of the event.

Around the Sambadrome I recall observing vignette scenes of people in fantastical costumes lying exhausted in the road at 4am, or a metro full of people in sequinned and tall feather-adorned costumes. The Sambadrome atmosphere was like a cross between a major sporting event and a 1930s Nazi rally. One float was disturbingly adorned in swastikas. The singing by so many people was fantastic and the parades put to shame Busby Berkeley routines I had seen on TV. It was not hard therefore to get carried away with the wave of revelry and carnival atmosphere.

I had learned from my girlfriend Susan that it was easy to obtain work teaching English in Rio, so I visited Feedback, the English language teaching school where Susan worked. As soon as I opened my mouth to say hello, school staff asked if I would teach a conversation class that afternoon. They also offered me five hours work per week on Tuesdays and Thursdays. I had never taught in my life and therefore spent the afternoon nervously preparing ideas for that evening's lesson. Carnival and the Brazilian debt crisis seemed pretty good 'off the shelf' topics and were, as I soon found out in class, remarkably popular too. All the students were engaged. I also learned a lot about the students' interests during the 90-minute conversation. Sergio was a discographer (a person who catalogues records) for a local radio station. He approached me after the lesson, my first ever, and asked my opinion on whether he should have private lessons.

From the depths of my experience, I drew myself up to face him, and with the look and words of an old hand, agreed that it might be a good idea as he would get individual attention. With my weighty experience I suggested an hourly rate that might be appropriate. This was the start of my freelance teaching experience in Rio.

The school sent me on a training course for one week and it was there I learned the basics of teaching English. I also enrolled at a downtown English language teaching academy where I took another week's worth of lessons in teaching English as a foreign language. I found that using contemporary news journals such as Time and Newsweek offered ways that I could start a conversation with my students, engaging them in conversations about issues of the day.

I could also be entirely natural in conversation class and simply relate everyday experiences and ask the class to offer information about their daily routines. For instance, I was stuck in the elevator between floors at the language academy one day and had to climb out between floors with the other passengers. The story provided entertaining raw material for my conversation class that evening. The students responded with their engaging tales of similar troublesome experiences.

I also related a story about trying to buy quejo (cheese) for lunch. Brazil uses the metric system of kilograms and grams for weight. I was used to the British imperial system of pounds and ounces and therefore had no appreciation of weight or volume, and being somewhat cautious in my early Rio days asked of the store if I could buy one gram of cheese for lunch. The storekeeper's eyes opened wide as he exclaimed that one gram of cheese would not provide a satisfying lunch as it amounted to about a quarter of a teaspoon. I was still new to Brazil, and I had much to learn.

After a while I worried about my ability to conduct conversation classes. I found it difficult to initiate an animated conversation between three, four or more, albeit educated, people from different interest areas, and maintain a lively discussion. The students though were fascinated with topics concerning the United States. President Reagan's post-Irangate speech/press conference provided excellent conversation material. When I built up confidence, I found I could have an educated and largely informed open discussion on contemporary issues: on American foreign policy, Democrats versus Republicans or the economic policies of Brazil, conversation that was both cultured and educated.

The main Rio carnival events take place across one week, with the final parade and samba school finals occurring on the Saturday, one week after I arrived. I arranged to attend the Sambadrome again. The first bloco (literally, street block samba school) passed. I felt the event did not carry the same level as excitement as the previous Saturday. It was amazing nonetheless for its infectious and repetitive drumming rhythms. Two people in the party I was with spoke Portuguese and English, so I could listen to translations of most of the ceremony proceedings and song lyrics.

At 9.30pm the second bloco came along. Breaks between the various parades averaged 30 or 40 minutes, but the time passed quickly in the warm, friendly atmosphere. The terraces filled as more carnivallers arrived at the Sambadrome. By midnight the main samba schools arrived for the parade. I felt that nothing, just nothing, could compare to this samba spectacle – without doubt it was the greatest show on earth.

The floats were huge, and built on enormous, wheeled chassis. Some were more political than would have been allowed just two or three years previously. Floats depicted the current realities of life in Brazil. One mocked the discredited Cruzado Plan, an economic plan introduced in 1986 and designed to stem inflation. Even street cleaners took part in the parades. Complete with brushes and dust carts they moved in unison, cleaning up the papers and streamers that were being constantly hurled into the parade pathway. They received the same level of applause as the beautiful girls and the other floats, and this cleaning up operation was turned into a working-class parade.

The big samba schools took over one hour to pass and the floats became ever more fantastical as the night continued. There were floats with roller skater dancers and a fountain that worked. Carnival surpassed any theatrical experience I had enjoyed in England.

I had planned to stay in Brazil for six weeks, so how much money I could earn remained a critical factor. I calculated the amount of private teaching work I needed to do to survive for six weeks. I would need ten hours at 150Cz$ per hour to get by, on a budget of 1500Cz$ per week. Of course, that also depended on inflation, which was then running at a crazy 20% per month. This inflation contributed to the confusing changes in Brazilian currency at that time. In 1987 it was the Cruzado, which had been introduced the year before. The Cruzado wouldn't last long. There were several more currency changes each designed to cope with the mad inflation until the Real was introduced in 1994 and is still in use today. Anyhow, on this budget and with the cash I had brought from England, I felt it might be possible to survive a total of nine weeks.

One of my private students, who had a plush apartment in Copacabana, was in novelty materials production, the kind of items they made for Carnival, using silver thread and silver laminated plastic materials. His motivation for learning English was so he could sell his materials in the United States. As he explained, there was a market for it in the pre-election razzmatazz coming up to the 1988 presidential elections.

After carnival, and on weekends in Rio, when I wasn't teaching, I visited various sites and parks in the city. One such one was Jardin Botanico, Rio's botanical garden. It was beautifully peaceful and cool, with a staggering array of tropical palms, plants, and squirrels. There were breadfruit trees, cocoa, jackfruit and many other fruit trees. Air plants, of the type I had seen in garden shops in England, grew abundantly as parasites on the trees and shrubs.

I also visited towns outside Rio like Petropolis, a mountain town about 90 minutes away by bus. It was the one-time home and summer palace of former Brazilian emperor, Dom Pedro. The Imperial Palace is so perfectly preserved you must wear special shoes to avoid damaging the floors. The climate here was much cooler than in Rio, particularly when the sun went down in the evening.

Back in Rio, one afternoon during my early days there, I met an American computer expert, Bernard James, a fellow teacher. The man was so clearly brilliant. He claimed to have worked on the Apollo space mission. Our conversation developed into a theory of how socialism and capitalism are old C19th ideas and not serving us very well today. Feeling so fully burned out from England's unpleasant doses of the same, I was captivated by the discussion. Bernard referred to 'zeitgeist', or the new spirit of the age that was developing to replace the old political formats. It was an intense conversation that at one point was attended by a Peruvian Inca lookalike man. A bizarre combination of people had gathered to discuss such complex global, social, agricultural and philosophical matters in such an unlikely setting. I felt excited and mentally drained by the conversation. The conversation led me and a fellow teacher to briefly explore the possibility of promoting in Brazil a thousand-year-old agricultural method of double digging agriculture, as a way of making farming methods more efficient and productive.

Rio was a troubled place during this period. One night, Central Station was nearly destroyed, and many people were injured, as a group of commuters attacked the train station in response to a train strike. The railways were just one of the many industries that had been affected by strikes. 'Estamos em Greve' (We are on Strike) was a familiar newspaper headline.

Rio is a beautiful city with spectacular scenery and exquisite women. Body beautiful reigns supreme. But, like the currency, a parallel black market exists in Rio. The alternative side of Rio is the robbers, prostitutes, transvestites, transsexuals, murderous bus drivers and the awful smell of urine. As I was sitting on the balcony of the Hotel Gloria, overlooking the Guanabara Bay, and looking across to Niteroi with Sugar Loaf Mountain on the right, it was almost impossible to reconcile the two sides of Rio – 'Cidade Marvelhosa' and 'Cidade Peligoso', the 'Marvellous City' and the 'Dangerous City'.

During the Easter period I decided to escape from the beauty and danger of Rio and explore some jungle beaches and countryside south of the city. The bus journey from Rio to Parati, some 258 km south of Rio, was spectacular – a coastal road with views across to the hundreds of large and small jungle islands. Deserted and near-deserted beaches appeared plentiful. Parati is close to the heart of Brazil's Atlantic's rain forest. The bay by Parati has views across to these islands.

I had been nervous about not being able to find accommodation. The alternative was to sleep outside, and risk being mugged, or eaten alive by mosquitos. You are always on your guard in Brazil against the Ledroa, the thief, who might just slash your bag or pull a knife on you and take everything you have. It was with some relief therefore that Parati appeared to be a safe vacation respite.

After wandering the streets, eventually I found 'Johnny Gringos', an amazing, dark and cavernous place where they spoke some English. Unfortunately, it was 'Completo'. Just around the corner though was 'Santa Anita', a cafe and hotel. It was a little expensive maybe at 600Cz$ per night but a good find. I took it immediately and only then began to relax. A cerveja (beer) later and I felt I could almost be in some tranquil Greek town. The calmness of the place after Rio was most welcome.

The sea around Parati glistened as suspended particles of brightly coloured minerals reflected the tropical sun like so many flakes of gold. The town beach was surrounded by jungle, palm trees, almond trees and a million other species of vegetation. There was a swamp complete with cranes and vultures.

It was Good Friday and as I looked out of the hotel window, I saw an Easter procession leading past the hotel. A beaten metal cross, some five feet high, and draped with a band of white cotton was held high at the front of the procession. People carrying white candles followed while a dreary and melancholy silver band kept a sort of pace. They filed through the narrow stone-slabbed streets to the church where they held Easter Mass.

Before I had left Rio for this Easter vacation, my friend Susan introduced me to an Englishman who owned a yacht. He was looking for crew to help him on his sail back to England from Rio, on the final leg of a round-the-world trip. The route was to be via the northern coast of Brazil, Trinidad, the Caribbean, and the Azores. He planned to be back in England by August or September 1987.

I was loving living and teaching in Rio but the prospect of crewing a boat from Rio through the south Atlantic and Caribbean was an equally tempting experience. The heat, the tropical scenery and wild ambience of this small holiday town provided a perfect setting to decide about my future.

This quiet time provided me with an opportunity to analyse my desires and life goals. Perhaps for the first time, I was able to lay out my goals and desires honestly. I did so by drawing up a list of pros and cons of remaining in Rio or traveling back to England by boat. I gave each pro and con item a one-to-five-point mark and added up the points as though to arrive at a scientific answer to my predicament. Realizing that this was no way to assess my life goals, I made the decision to go with my gut feelings. I opted for the boat journey as offering a unique experience, one that I could probably never replicate later in life. I said goodbye to fellow travellers in the hotel and learned a new word, 'saudade' which means a deep longing or a missing. I would miss Rio; I would miss those spontaneous conversations in the hotel about the best place to buy pirated goods or get a hair transplant or inexpensive dental work, and I would miss my students.

I still wanted to travel further in Brazil before leaving the country and so I arranged to meet the boat and crew in Salvador, Bahia about a day or more's drive from Rio. I handed in my notice to the school, said goodbye to my private students and headed north on a bus to Salvador on the Eastern coast of central Brazil.

Salvador is a very different place from Rio. People have a much darker skin because of their African heritage; it is less cosmopolitan and western tourists and travellers are more conspicuous. Candomblé is the local religion, one based upon the practice of tribal chants and special gods. The means of survival for many young people in this city is a daily devotion and total allegiance to Capoeria (see my explanation of this below). That, coupled with the usually friendly but sly way of living off tourists and travellers for sex and money, gives Salvador a grubby likability. Salvador is a strangely wonderful and unsettling town. Within one hour of arriving, I met two friendly local Capoeira dancers from the square who took me and Susan, who had agreed to accompany me on my trip to Salvador, to nearby Itapuã beach, a palm-filled sandy beach with a largo or lake nearby.

I found Salvador to be an exquisitely exotic place. The following day I took a trip around the Praça de Sé area in the centre of town. In the afternoon, I returned to the beach at Itapuã where I bathed in a warm water lagoon. By the side of the lagoon, I saw 'gente pobre', poor people who washed clothes and dried them on the nearby sand dunes.

The Capoeira dance is a form of Angolan foot fighting that has since developed into an energetic acrobatic dance, often performed to the accompaniment of the berimbau, a stringed instrument plucked by a stone. Capoeira seemed to be the main occupation for many young people in Salvador. Many made a living from it, either by taking donations from tourists, or by teaching it at dance schools in the area. One might compare it to the rap music or drumming heard in many US cities. It is an urban culture practised by a young and poor population.

My last days in Salvador flickered past like images from a cartoon movie, so vivid and larger than life. The South African political and religious leader, Bishop Desmond Tutu, arrived in Pelourinho Square in the old city centre to deliver an anti-apartheid message to Salvador, Bahia. An oppressed and 80% black population was well in tune with what he had to say.

The square was not packed, though there were perhaps 500 people assembled for the event. The stage was constructed of rudimentary scaffolding and boards, and the part where Tutu was to speak had a corrugated roof above it. In true press fashion, the handkerchief-sized space was crawling with photographers, hanging on like lichen or those parasitic plants that cling to trees in the tropics. Naturally, the view for the rest of us was utterly obscured. Still, the occasional glimpse of purple cloth up there on the stage did provide the impression that a bishop was indeed present.

"Blacks will not be free until the whites are also free," Tutu said, to some applause and some mixed reaction. It was clearly a historic occasion for Salvador, though – and so special for the poverty-stricken area of Pelourinho.

That evening a Festa was held. It may have been a special feast day, or just perhaps because Bishop Desmond Tutu had visited, I wasn't sure. The well-known Brazilian singer Gilberto Gil performed. It seemed that much of the concert was mobile, a travelling show consisting of the singer delivering Bahian reggae sounds to a regular drum beat while sitting on top of a set of speakers which had been loaded onto a Volkswagen open truck.

Our Capoeira friends and I were well stocked with beer, and we sat down in a grassy area to enjoy the music and the festive atmosphere. It was late, close to midnight. We saw police trucks drive around the grassy area that we had taken over as our own. The police shouted at us. I had no idea what they were saying, but they directed us into the back of their open-air truck. There didn't seem to be much choice about how that evening was going to develop. The truck stopped at the police station, and we were hustled inside and downstairs to the jail. I looked at my friends one last time before we were each directed into single cells. I was due to meet my sailing friends at the port the next morning. Jail-time was an unexpected and rather worrying development.

My cell was dark except for some light that came through the metal bars. I had a concrete bunk bed but no blanket or pillow. I also had a terrible headache due to an overabundance of drinks. I feared I had just become a Midnight Express casualty and wondered if I was going to be in a Brazilian jail for months or years.

I had picked up some Portuguese and desperately attempted to communicate with my jailed neighbour. I tapped on the pipes that ran along the ceiling, hoping to find a kindred and English-speaking spirit. While I did hear noises and voices, nothing provided answers to my predicament, so I settled as best I could on the concrete bunk, hoping to at least rid myself of the headache. I couldn't sleep though, and kept my eyes strained through the darkness to anything that might provide a clue to what might happen next. At 6 am, a guard woke me and escorted me upstairs to what was clearly the office of the head policeman. I had no expectation of what might come next, so I was relieved to hear that he was simply interested in who I was, where I came from and what I thought of Brazil. We never did hear why the police held us overnight. Perhaps we had broken curfew. I never knew, but the incident became one of many tales I would get to tell. I had a spring in my step as I exited the police station and headed back to the room where we had been staying, to collect my few belongings, ready for the journey ahead.

I was almost ready to leave Bahia. I only needed to extend my visa. I said goodbye to a fellow traveller at the top of the city elevator that divides the upper and lower towns and descended to the next part of my voyage.

At Sea

'The Northanger' was a 43-foot hand-built, steel-hulled yacht constructed and designed by Rick, the captain. Living quarters were cramped, consisting of a small dining area, galley, navigation table, bunks for four people and two double-bed cabins. My fellow crew included Irwin, a German school teacher; Toby, an

Northanger Boat moored in Natal for repairs – on the boat L, Irwin, R, Toby

English physicist researcher who became part of the crew after working in Antarctica at the British Antarctic Survey; Susan, my girlfriend, plus Rick, the captain, and Rebecca, his girlfriend. We were all young, in our early 30s.

Having never been sailing, I had some romantic idea that I might learn something. The route up the northeast coast of Brazil and up to the Caribbean was something I had only dreamed of or read about.

After 48 hours of not knowing whether my stomach contents were staying put or going out to sea for a little sail of their own, I gradually adjusted to the constant motion of the boat. We awoke on the first full day of sailing to the spectacular sight of a shoal of one hundred or more dolphins all breaching at our bow. Such intelligent creatures they are, that they all decided to tag us for several hours in a spirit of welcome to the South Atlantic.

The sea was calm in the early days of our voyage. Often, we had to have the motor running because there wasn't enough wind to keep the sails full. The boat had two sails, a staysail and a genoa that bowed out when we had wind giving the fanciful impression of being carried along by a great white bird.

The boat averaged 165 to 170 miles per day at a steady nine knots. We sailed from Salvador to the northeast port of Natal, a journey by sea of a few days. After restocking the boat with fresh fruit and vegetables, and having explored the nearby sand dunes and beaches, we set sail once more. The journey from Natal to Trinidad would take 14 days, five of which would be in the Doldrums.

I felt my bunk had to be the smallest place I had ever existed in. It was wide at the top for the shoulders and tapered off sharply for the torso and legs. I christened it 'The coffin'. On one side of the bed were deep shelves for my belongings. On the other, a board to stop me falling on to Irwin, a chirpy 24-year-old German crew member who lay below. Irwin had joined the boat back in Rio and had sailed to Salvador. His voracious appetite sharply contrasted with mine. His early morning quest for eggs, fried potatoes and tomatoes stood alongside my, later in the day, weak slurps of light soup or fruit salad, as testament to the fact he had ten days' sailing experience before me.

There were six people crewing the boat. Being a crew member was not too onerous. Our main duties were 'watches'. Watches were evenly divided between the crew. Mine were 9 to 12, morning and night. Watches could be wonderfully pleasant on calm days and grossly uncomfortable when the sea became rough.

Toby had just finished a two-year stretch in the Antarctic working for the British Antarctic Survey. I learned that the Survey existed on £12 million per year. Toby had studied physics before leaving England for the Antarctic. His job had been to conduct experiments, monitor the atmosphere and, on days off, observe penguins or fish. There was little else to do in the barren landscape, he explained.

The variety of food we had on the boat was extraordinary, although there was no refrigeration on board. Much of the food was tinned or dried and had been brought over from New Zealand. It was stowed in the hull below the cabin floor to keep it cool. There were tins of sardines, corned beef, corned lamb, sweetcorn, and tomatoes. We even had tinned butter and dried whole milk. Rebecca, the captain's girlfriend, made fresh bread and yoghurt daily. She also provided an assortment of dried beans and pulses. The combination of these items in creative combinations provided us with very nourishing meals. As I reflect on this, I am sure we fared better on this voyage than my theatre colleague, Captain James Cook, on his scurvy-ridden excursions.

During my night watches, I wrote. Writing by moonlight, masked by the sails, can only be done by feel. You can't see what you're writing or check that you've put a comma in the right place, crossed your Ts or dotted your Is. The weathervane, incorporating an automatic steering system, was usually turned on. It relieved crew members from having to steer for hours at a time, and it helped us maintain our course. With a constant wind, there was precious little to do on a night watch. We were sailing some 300 miles east from any land mass. There were no boats this far out, only the constant motion of the sea and the pinprick lights from the stars. The Southern Cross was visible, and so too the Plough. Shooting stars were plentiful as they streaked across the vastness of the sky.

Time passed remarkably quickly each day. The watches broke up the day, and the rest of the time was spent sleeping, washing and reading. Washing was fun. Up on deck, you secure a rope tied to a bucket, strip down and trail the bucket in the sea, which in that part of the world at that time of year was a pleasant 28 degrees C. Regular shampoo forms a generous lather in salt water and provided you dry yourself with a towel immediately, the salt doesn't crystalize on your body. 'Showers' were a public affair, usually conducted right in the line of view of whoever was steering the boat.

One time we believed we had crossed the equator. There, of course, had been no visible line in the ocean. It was cool and cloudy. We didn't even feel a 'bump'. Nor was there a flurry of flying fish, looking ridiculous as they can do, aimlessly skimming between the waves. Like foolish aquarian lemmings, with not a thought for where they're going, some would land on the deck where they lay hopelessly basking in the midday sun until they dried brittle.

It was all an error, however. We didn't cross the equator. Rick and Irwin's sextant sightings of the stars confirmed it. I felt a little heartened to be still travelling in the southern hemisphere. Frankly, after watching the water go down the plughole anti-clockwise, I was in no rush to fall back into the ways of the north too soon.

Our physicist companion, Toby, told us that the path taken by water down a plughole is not affected by one's hemispherical position and that many other forces come to bear on the passage of water in such confines. Such forces, he explained, depend partly on the way you pull the plug out of the sink, the bore of the pipe, the stability of the sink unit, and other variable factors. I understand today, however, that the confounding plughole theory continues to be a source of constant speculation in the physics community.

During much of the boat journey, I anxiously monitored the shortwave radio for news of the British election. It may sound surprising to have maintained an interest in British politics while in the middle of the Southern Ocean, but I was aware that the outcome of the election could have a bearing on the job market back home. During the period leading up to the election, the BBC's World Service had lined up a series of news analyses and commentary, heartlessly sweeping aside merchant shipping news, *Tales from the Countryside* and other programming delights that normally kept us at one with the rest of humanity. We were all glued to the shortwave radio set as we glided smoothly past Suriname and out of the Doldrums.

Reading was another way of passing the time on the boat. I read *Castaway*, an account of a young woman who spent her life living and surviving on a deserted tropical island. She had been attracted by a classified ad in the newspaper to marry and spend time with a man on a tropical island. The marriage turned out to be disastrous, the man left her, and she learned how to survive on fruit and fish. I also read *Who Sank the Rainbow Warrior*, an account of the explosion aboard the Greenpeace boat that had been moored in New Zealand. It was alleged that the explosives had been set by the French secret service. I also read Ted Simon's *Jupiter's Travels*, an account of his four-year journey around the world on a motorbike. I mused that these are the kind of books that make the most sense to read when you are in the middle of the South Atlantic.

At last, positively sweltering heat confirmed that we had crossed the equator. Star sightings provided that extra scientific proof.

It was another beautiful and calm night when this milestone occurred. I sat on deck and listened as the wisps of gentle wind allowed the sails to lapse into momentary sleep before they crashed nervously back into position on the upturn of the wave and reassumed their natural bowed shape.

The moon popped out from between the clouds like a half-chewed mint sweet to reflect its splendour on the sea below. I had noticed earlier that evening that the best time to view sunsets is not the actual time they go down but the 'after-sunset' – the half-hour period after the sun has sunk beneath the waves. That is the time to watch. The sky turns mauve with the last patches of daylight blue, the whole being subtlety reflected against the quiet ocean.

It was staggeringly difficult to believe that anything could change on the horizon out here, 300 miles from land. The wind stayed constant. There was never a change of scenery. We always steered 350 degrees.

We experienced just twenty-four hours of Doldrums, the low-pressure equatorial band of climate. I had in mind that the South Atlantic would bring raging seas, storms, thunder, and spray cascading over the bows. As it turned out, it was glassy seas and a total absence of wind which required the motor to be on for the entire period.

One trick to try when the boat was going slow was to throw a rope over the back of the boat, ensuring, of course, one end is firmly secured to the boat. The idea then is to clamber down the back of the boat and drop into the 28-degree C water, grip the rope, and be towed along behind. You get a very pleasurable effect as the water travels from your torso and through your loins. To aid in washing, you can soap yourself down first and have your body cleaned to a whisker. It is like a maritime car wash but for human bodies.

The first few moments of this escapade can indeed be pleasurable. But then, when your arms begin to ache, and you get the feeling of not being able to hold on, panic can swiftly set in, and you dearly wish you weren't being dragged through the sea in this ungainly manner. Your whole mouth fills up with water, and soon you feel you can't get back to the boat. You then look up to the boat as though for help. If everyone looks normal and unconcerned, you suffer alone in these circumstances. With supreme determination, you can drag yourself back to the boat using the rope. You then clamber aboard and, with the agility of a beached whale, recover. I was shaking for half an hour after this ordeal and decided not to repeat the experience.

Rick, the captain, informed us one day that we were each using six litres of water per day which was ridiculous. I felt guilty as I thought of the times I had rinsed my hair in fresh water after a seawater shower or cooked potatoes in fresh water. I wondered how much I used at home each day.

And so, it came to the final days of the gruelling and often exasperating 1,900-mile, two-week voyage to Trinidad. It was exasperating because of the sheer length of time being tossed from one side of the boat to the other. It was exasperating, too, because of the heat. At night, with the hatches down because of the rain or waves which would often splash onto the deck, the boat became an insufferable sweat box.

June 11, 1987, it was a Thursday and the day of the Great British General Election. There was a full moon and an energetic sea. Squally rain and high but not quite raging seas made it distinctly uncomfortable in the cabin downstairs. All this contributed toward the foreboding of a Tory win. They did, of course, for the third successive time, and the crowing of Margaret Thatcher on the World Service afterwards seemed so appallingly real even there in the middle of the South Atlantic. I wondered what I might return to if I did go back to England.

At night, Trinidad is visible from about 40 miles away on the sea, from the southeast. The flares from oil fields cast an ethereal glowing light on the clouds above the horizon. We rounded the southwest coast, which was dark and a seemingly uninhabited terrain from our distance of one to two miles from land. Signs of life were apparent, though as we spotted human refuse floating by the boat's hull. These were murky waters.

The northern coast and entrance bay to Port of Spain, the capital of Trinidad, is littered with little islands and dangerous rocks. Port of Spain lay a little over five miles away. While steering by moonlight, we maintained a wide course to avoid the rocks. This meant we had to sail almost to the Venezuelan coast before entering Boca de Dragon, the impressive name given to the bay leading to the island's capital.

What the people were like, and the country, had almost no place in my mind at this point. Uppermost was that I could finally wash out sheets, all but cracked from dried-in dirt and equatorial sweat. I was, peculiarly, therefore, in no rush to leave the boat until my tiny but important bunk terrain had been cleaned.

The harbour in Port of Spain is no picturesque scene. Pelicans vie with ferries and the polluted waters. Surprisingly, as I later learned, fish do frequent the waters. Rick and Rebecca returned to the boat, having acquainted themselves with the customs' authorities.

I recall thinking about the idea of customs and its meaning to a country. I think that the term customs embraces so many things about a country, not solely related to trade but to culture and the way of doing things. It seems right that when you cross into another country other than your own, you must enter a portal of authority that addresses some element of these things.

I found it surprisingly easy to adjust mentally to another currency, Trinidadian dollars. My maritime companions and I explored the town, ending up at the Savannah, an open common just north of the centre. As we sipped fresh coconut juice, we spoke with local vendors. They told us about venues where we could hear calypso and steel band music. David Rudder, a well-known calypso singer, was to be playing nearby one evening during our stay in Trinidad.

Trinidad is a marvellously colourful and friendly country with a rich culture and distinctive rhythms. Now it only has a hint of its former British dominance. White walls, dusty streets, colonial style government buildings and the sweaty ambience of the place were a friendly alternative to the often-dangerous streets of Rio and the boredom of the boat.

Ten days passed by quickly. There were discos and bars to visit and steel bands to hear. I recall a memorable taxi trip around the island that took us from a lunch of home cooking out in the jungle to a pitch lake in the town of La Brea where pitch literally oozes from the ground. Trinidad exports this tar pitch to help build roads in Australia and Africa.

Like all 'seasoned' sailors we had to move on. I felt a real sadness as we sailed away from Trinidad. I felt the other Caribbean islands would pale in comparison, not in scenic beauty, but in life and people.

The journey to Grenada took about thirty hours. At a bearing of perhaps 30 degrees, that meant sailing against the waves. As most sailors would know, this meant the boat had to attempt to splice its way against mother nature. And for this maritime arrogance, mother nature imparts its revenge. Symptoms veer from constant but unproductive retching to bruised flesh and severely stubbed limbs as one tries to manoeuvre a passage above or below deck. This unhappy combination was not conducive to a dream-filled slumber or a fresh daily awakening. I was grateful the sail was so short.

Grenada is surely a jewel in the ocean, a luscious island sparkling at us as we glided in at noon after a vicious sail. The routine we had been accustomed to at landing was to draw in and neatly lay out the anchor chain in the bow, and haul down, fold, and put covers over the sails to protect them from the strong sunlight. Smaller sails, like the genoa, were bagged and placed on top of the anchor chain in the bow. Finally, the dinghy was lowered into the clear water. The design of the boat, with its keel that could be raised into the centre of the boat, allowed us to moor very close to shore.

It had been three years since the Americans invaded Grenada and three years since the tiny island had been swathed in global publicity. I was anxious to explore. "We cleared all the Marxists out!" our genial driver said as we drove up from the beach, landing into St. George's, the capital. The first stop when we reached land was always the bank. I followed this routine with a visit to the consulate, where I caught up with the news from Britain. You can read the London *Times* or *Daily Telegraph* until noon at the British consulate in St George's.

The harbour in St. George's is exquisitely cluttered by fishing boats, ferries, yachts and haulage vessels, all coexisting in a happy lazy medium delineated by the curved bay-side promenade. Mini cabs are the preferred mode of transport in the Caribbean. Their drivers entice you inside with "cheaper than his" deals and crush 12 to 15 people inside before they let loose a deadly beat-box rhythm of reggae and steel from the wizard interior sound system. It's a fine scheme.

Eager to learn more about the island and be at one with its culture I visited the local museum in St. George's. It houses a store of documents and artefacts that chart Grenada's history, from the French and English battles in the C16th and C17th, to the 1984 rise and fall of Maurice Bishop, the former Grenadian leader. From the photographs and newspaper articles, it seemed clear that Bishop was a popular leader and that his assassin had aimed to form a hard-left government after Bishop's assassination.

While it appeared many local people still mourned the loss of Bishop, from my studies at the museum and conversations with residents, they felt glad the United States had intervened. Grenada though, despite the American intervention was at that time by no means a bustling economy, and there were no visible signs of US economic aid other than a new airport. The main trade then was still spices like nutmeg and mace.

There were a few American entrepreneurs though. One we met had developed a way of cultivating mushrooms under banana leaves. We also met the manager of Cable and Wireless, the telecommunications company that was providing for much of the inter-island's telephone communications. We accompanied this telecom leader to the island's main communications tower high in the country's mountain jungle.

It was here that the so-called telephone hotline between the United States and Grenada had been established. I was staggered by the crudity of the structure that housed the hotline, as well as the complete absence of security. It seemed so easy for anyone to disrupt the life of these islands by taking over a just a few strategic positions.

Dave, the Cable & Wireless manager, seemed clearly in command of his job, which entailed maintaining genial relations with the local politicians and island community. To maintain good relations with the community, the company sponsored a local cricket team and, in the process, helped preserve a little bit more of the British Commonwealth. For all this, Dave complained he still felt he was an outsider. Yet here we were, Susan, Irwin, Toby, and I, in the peak years of the Reagan administration, being privy to the mechanics of international relations. I was not impressed!

We stayed in Grenada for ten days. It was something of a shock to realize that time passed out here. Carriacou lay just over 20 miles north of Grenada, a mere five or six hours sail away. That island was our next sailing stopover. Rick, the captain, had by now set his sights on heading north as quickly as possible, to avoid the hurricane season. He sailed the boat up a hurricane hole as soon as we reached Carriacou.

Carriacou is blessed with three desert islands sitting serenely off the coast. The island had a healthy boatbuilding and fishing community. It had suffered little from tourism and small wonder, I thought, as I looked at its pocket-sized airplane landing strip off the main road leading into town. Boats would bring fresh fruit and vegetables from Grenada once a week and a crowd gathered each time a new shipment came in.

I learned a little more about the American invasion of Grenada and the events that had led up to it from a woman that ran a harbour-side cafe. She said that the Marxists had buried guns and ammunition in the hills and the Americans had discovered the arms cache. This was not much to go on, but it seemed to add some justification to the US-led invasion.

After Carriacou, we sailed on to a nearby deserted island about 15 miles north. It was very rocky. Irwin, Toby and I braved the steep slopes, and the bush, for a cross-island excursion. The island was only one mile wide. As we reached the furthest side, we were rewarded by the sight of a small fishing community of perhaps 20 people. One of the villagers sold us some Belgian beer. We thought it strange that he was able to come by such things. He explained that, with a boat and outboard motor, it was possible to sail to Grenada in only two hours. They were able to buy all they needed from Grenada and bring it back to the village. The villagers also gave us some of the juiciest mangoes I have ever tasted. The flesh of the fruit melted as it entered our mouths. The fishermen took us to see their boats and we helped them haul one out of the sea. Afterwards, we returned to the trail and back over the hill to our boat.

Meanwhile, while Toby and I had been exploring the island, the Northanger had gained neighbours, a German couple with whom Irwin naturally made acquaintance. This chance meeting led us to surely the most beautiful and deserted part of the Caribbean waters, Tobago. Without a boat, don't even hope to get there!

Tobago Cays is a group of palm-dressed, sandy islands, abundant in coral and piles of sun-bleached washed and dried conch shells. The islands lie in the heart of the southern Caribbean. The sea was clear and warm. I had been tardy about going full sportsman-like into the ocean depths for fear of unknown creatures lurking in the dark seaweed. But here, since the water was so clear to 30 to 50 feet, diving with a snorkel into the 28-degree waters was like returning to the womb. I felt so at ease with the surroundings.

From being a nervous surface swimmer, I quickly adapted to being a water baby. The natural sculptures of the coral were just as I had seen in Jacques Cousteau's films. I could swim and drift for hours just gazing at the blue Angel fish and the many thousands of multi-coloured shoals of fish that artfully glide from one coral cove to another. I carefully watched what I touched and was thankful for gloves as some coral can be razor sharp. My only moment of panic came when I spotted a Scorpionfish swimming toward me. I knew their bite to be poisonous.

We sailed out of the Tobago after a few hours for a final two-day journey to Antigua. It was during this last sail that I was beginning to get a better feel for the geography of the northern Caribbean Sea. We sailed gracefully past all the main Winward Islands as well as St Vincent. I wished that we could have stopped because

St Vincent had a carnival that weekend. St. Vincent claims its carnival tops that of Rio. You can hear the same claim though in Trinidad and the other islands. I had by this time become accustomed to these claims and took each with, as they say, a pinch of salt.

We also sailed by St. Lucia, Martinique, Dominique (Dominica), and Guadeloupe. At Dominique, we were treated to the sight of the capital city at night. As we sailed within three miles of the island, we could easily hear the distant sounds of the traffic in the city.

We sighted the coast of Antigua at 8:00 am the next morning. It was my last watch on the vessel that had been my home for two months. Somehow, I didn't feel impassioned or even sad as I steered the boat into the harbour on my last leg northwards.

I had developed a laziness of mind and temperament throughout the last months in the surprisingly emotionally sheltered environment on the sea. There had been no raging seas, and the challenge had not been one of a daring adventure of survival but of a man in a mist of sun and time.

There were few responsibilities on the boat, except to do your watch, and in mild seas and with an automatic steering system, this wasn't difficult. My travel companion, Irwin, and I revelled in our freedom as we lowered our bags into the dingy. Susan and Irwin were to travel with Rick and Rebecca to England. We said our goodbyes to Susan, Rick, Rebecca and Toby, and rowed to shore. I looked out over the bay as the Northanger sailed toward the horizon. We both watched the boat until we could only see a tiny spot on the horizon.

Irwin and I found a room in English Harbour, one of the main towns on the island, on the waterfront. There was a living room with two beds, a bathroom, and a small stove. After settling into our newly found land-based abode, we set out to discover whatever may lie ahead on this island. As we walked along the road into town, we spotted a pizza bar. We stopped in for a coffee and a slice. We asked the pizza bar owner if there were any interesting events on the island that we could attend. He told us that Eric Clapton was playing there tonight at 7 pm. Assuming this was a joke, we nonetheless made plans to return to the pizza bar at 7 pm that evening. We located seats by the bar and sure enough, around 7:30 pm, in walked Eric Clapton and Jools Holland. Irwin and I spent this extraordinary evening in this tiny space listening to 'Lay Lady Lay', 'Wonderful Tonight', 'I Shot the Sheriff' and other Clapton classics while Jools played keyboards. We could only conclude that these kinds of events were a normal occurrence in this part of the world. I later learned that many British and American rock musicians spent their summers in the Caribbean playing small venues.

So, what became of my sailing companions? Sadly, Rick died a few years later, trying one last rock climb by the Northwest Passage. It turned out that the main purpose of the boat for him had always been to access some amazing climbs. Toby and Susan, I never saw again nor Rebecca. I last saw Irwin as he headed west along 59th Street in New York. Being cooped up together for a long time on a boat at sea creates a rare bond, and that group of people carries strong and special memories that I still cherish.

I had plotted a variety of exotic routes back to civilization before we chose to buy a flight from Antigua to San Juan, Puerto Rico, and from San Juan to New York City. I had met a woman, Julie, in Antigua for barely ten minutes while cashing a cheque at the bank. She gave me the name of a friend, Gene, who could put me up in New York. When I arrived in New York, Gene said that any friend of Julie was a friend of his, and he provided me with hospitality and accommodation for one week at his Manhattan apartment close to the United Nations building. I later admitted to Gene that Julie and I had met in Antigua for just 10 minutes!

From New York, I travelled to Washington DC. Robin, a friend I had worked with at the Half Moon Theatre, let me stay in her apartment until I could find accommodation of my own. It was always my intention to return to England. Apart from anything else, I reasoned that my clothes were there, not to say family, friends and a house in Stoke Newington, London, where I owed a share of the mortgage. I asked Robin if she knew of a way that I could make some money before I returned to England. Robin said she would introduce me to a fellow student of hers who was cold-calling radio stations to offer short-form programmes.

CHAPTER 5:
A NEW LAND

Radio Calling

When I joined North American Network, I found a company that had verve, ingenuity and drive. It was managed by a young person fresh from college. Bill, the owner and president, had a sense of running a business but little practical experience in all the business skills that would later be needed to develop the company into one that could be known and respected by radio stations, corporations and public relations agencies. I felt my experience and skills in theatre sales and media management could be of value. Bill thought so too and offered me a job as Station Services Manager. My job was to be responsible for marketing to radio stations all programmes developed by the company. I was also charged with the responsibility of providing broadcast reports to programme sponsors.

At this time, the company was distributing a series of consumer lifestyle tips programmes that were sponsored by US corporations. It was soft advertising, and I was initially turned off by the company's reference to the distribution of radio 'shows'. My background in the theatre had taught me to reserve the term 'show' for a more theatrically creative meaning. My job was to encourage radio station programmers to air the material for free on their stations. The method chosen to accomplish this function was telemarketing.

In the early weeks of telemarketing, I was provided a list of stations to call. After a while, it became clear to me that these lists were recording information about station responses in random order. During a workday, I may start talking to a radio station in Alpena, MI, and the next station on my list was in Boston, MA, the next in Salina, CA, and then back to Alpena to talk to the FM sister station of the AM one which had the same call letters and the same programme director. This organizational approach made little sense, and I looked earnestly in the direction of the source from which these random lists emerged, a green screen IBM PC. Remember, back then, there were no neat Excel spreadsheets! I decided that, given the authority, I would do something to correct this inefficiency. I had already developed some sense of media lists in England during the Jarrow March. So, it was then, in the fading months of 1987, that I developed an interest in computers and databases.

I envisioned a computer system where not only could radio station information be logically ordered by state, radio station and audience size, but the information could be categorized to produce information only on those stations we needed at that specific time. I had experienced the value of computerized media lists during the Jarrow March, and so had some understanding of their value. It was only later that I realised what phenomenal power and competitive advantage a database could provide to an organisation.

To develop a telemarketing operation for the company, I had in mind a streamlined flow of information that emanated from the computer and was passed on to telemarketing staff, who then passed on and retrieved information from radio station programme directors that could be fed back into the computer, which could then produce mailing labels and later be used to provide broadcast information reports for programme sponsors.

All this represented quite a leap of coordination and efficiency for the company then. Previously, someone had been hired to type labels and produce broadcast reports by hand, thus repeating the recording and retrieval of the same pieces of information. I later realised, of course, that in this move to create an efficient system, I had developed a data processing monster that needed to be operated by human beings. The process of radio syndication became a matter of volume calling and data processing. Still, while I recognised the dulling effect that this had on the humans doing the job, I also recognised that we were getting results. The implications were that future staffing needs should take into account people with computer skills who were highly organised. I also recognized the value of linking telemarketing staff and the database via a local area network. The network would eliminate a data processing gridlock and avoid the need for printed call lists.

To develop the initial radio database system, I took such computerised information as the company had at the time and developed a relational database. I started by entering the call letters of every radio station in the US into Lotus 123. At the time, there were about 11,000 radio stations. After data-entering all 11,000 call letters, I became quite the authority on US stations. Lotus 123 was soon eclipsed in capability by Borland's Paradox database, a tool that I researched, learned and developed through scripting language to the point where it became a strategic asset to the company. I researched sources of radio station information, trained data entry staff, organized the entering of thousands of pieces of radio data and developed the system that, I'm proud to say, was only recently retired at the company.

I worked with North American Network in this station management position for two years, marketing radio programmes and reporting audience broadcast estimates to corporate sponsors.

During this period, I also scripted and produced a demo tape containing excerpts of the company's programming. I used the tape to attract affiliations from radio stations.

I lacked a trained background in broadcasting or radio, other than arranging press coverage for live events, and some studio and outside broadcasting experience learned through working at InterAction. I, therefore, took it upon myself to learn the broadcast business. I learned a good deal just by talking with hundreds of radio programme directors each day. I learned how programming decisions are made, all about different station formats and radio sales.

Through developing the radio database, I also learned a great deal about the locations of hundreds of US cities as well as their placement within recognised media markets. Through the additional reading of broadcast trade magazines and books, I learned about audience ratings, the role of the National Association of Broadcasters, the Radio Advertising Bureau, and the Federal Communications Commission. After 18 months, I had acquainted myself with a fair amount of broadcasting and syndication knowledge, and I wrote a short booklet on the state of radio and radio syndication for the company's internal use.

During the same period, I was also responsible for generating sales and selling programmes to corporations, trade associations, government agencies and public relations firms. By talking to public relations and product publicity staff at hundreds of organizations across America, I imbibed the essence of American consumerism and culture. Moving from a creative and uniquely British culture to one that commoditised everything with the sole aim of selling something to someone did not come easily to me. I knew, though, that what awaited me in England should I return, a life under Thatcher in a declining arts environment, was not a future for me either, so I relentlessly pursued the American dream.

I realised how travelling had taught me how to search for key information. When you are travelling and you enter a new town or country, there are a few essential items of information you need to survive. You need to find accommodation; you need to eat, and you ought to amass information about the town or country and its culture to not only survive but to make your stay in that place interesting and worthwhile. I used these same information-finding skills during my early days in Washington DC not only to survive but to develop and make a new career in broadcasting in the United States.

During this period, I hired an assistant and marketed an assortment of corporately sponsored short-form radio programmes. I helped develop the company's audio news release service, which provided a service to organisations that needed timely release of corporate news. The electronic news industry was just developing at this time, and we monitored the role of competitor organisations providing similar services in both radio and television, particularly the audio and video news release business.

Satellite distribution was a common way to distribute news to far-flung radio stations. You purchased time on the satellite service, placed your new story or sound bite and provided stations with the coordinates for them to download the story and air it locally. The system had inherent flaws, though, not least that stations had to proactively download your story, and you had no way of knowing if they did, or if they aired the piece. There had to be a better way.

One project that I could exercise previous experience in was trade show organisation. When the National Association of Broadcasters held their radio convention in Washington DC, it gave me an opportunity to promote the work of the company to a variety of radio programmers and allied broadcasting trades. Using my background in theatre, I hired a theatre designer to design and build the trade show booth. I used my experience with exhibition layout and booth management to plan, staff and manage the company's booth and presence at the convention.

I knew nothing about radio advertising, so when the company sold a cooperative advertising project to a trade association, the Outdoor Power Equipment Association, I was anxious to learn this aspect of the business. I immersed myself in the project, developing marketing materials and a marketing and station clearance strategy.

While North American Network had been successful in attracting corporate business, it was often business that was not retained. It had attempted to expand its operations by moving location from the conservative environs of downtown DC to the funkier neighbourhood of Adams Morgan. The company also hired three new staff. The influx of new staff, combined with an uncertain direction, led to a couple of senior members of the sales staff leaving, who then set up media relations firms that would compete for the same business as ours.

After this incident, I was asked to take over as director of sales for the company and to try to establish direction and sales momentum. I accepted the new position while also retaining overall responsibility for the station services department. I had monitored the role of the sales department during my time as station services manager and had recognized that the sales thrust of the company lacked any cohesive marketing strategy. I immediately set about implementing one. I also set up job descriptions as well as communications systems and procedures that would help clarify lines of responsibility.

Using my skills in database management, I established a sales and marketing database that would provide the information resources for an efficient marketing programme. The database would also provide a single source of information about accounts and customer histories, which had been lacking in the past. By centralising the accounts information, the database would also help avoid the errors of allowing individual sales staff to retain complete information on company accounts. I set about developing the sales and marketing database, also in Paradox, that would support marketing and corporate decision-making. Though I didn't perhaps realise it at the time, I was in command by then of a sales and media distribution resource that would become the foundation of the company's fortunes for decades to come.

I realised that overcoming some of the management burdens and lack of sales staff accountability of the past would not be easy, and I approached my task with considerable caution. I also knew that the marketing strategies I established would take time to develop and bear fruit. I had never been a director of sales and had much to learn about staff management and motivation.

In 1990 the company suffered from the departure of one of its principals, who had been responsible for much of the company's creative ideas and for establishing many of the company's most creative accounts. This had some effect on programme development, and I felt it incumbent upon myself to help fill some of the creative gaps caused by this staff departure.

The company had evolved by this time into an entity that was far more complex than its founder had originally envisaged. While the company's work encompassed radio syndication, its initial goal of becoming an independent radio network had not been realised. Instead, it had developed into a complex company that offered radio syndication as well as some of the more traditional public relations activities common to many PR agencies.

This complexity presented an identity crisis, both internally and externally. It became difficult to describe the role of the company to the outside world. If the company was to succeed, this identity crisis was a factor that needed to be addressed internally initially and then through a more sharply defined marketing programme.

While tackling some of these issues and managing sales staff, I also had to make sales of my own. One of these sales was to the National Education Association (NEA). I had been following President Bush's statements about being the 'education president' and the statements on education which he made at the National Governors Association meeting in Charlottesville at the latter end of 1989. I approached the NEA with the idea of a series of radio programmes and on-site coverage that would highlight the role the union was playing in the debate about the establishment of national goals for education. The NEA was excited by the idea, and I set up a series of teleconferenced interviews for the NEA president, Keith Geiger, timed to coincide with the next meeting of the National Governors Association.

I also arranged, as part of our contract with the NEA, to cover the National Governors Meeting in Washington and President HW 'elder' Bush's statements about being the education president. All this proved to be a great opportunity for me to get my feet wet in the Washington DC political scene.

In 1989, while on a business trip to New York, I learned about the tragic events in San Francisco caused by the earthquake, which killed 67 people and caused damage of more than $5 billion. As I watched the television reports, my boss Bill remarked to me that he wished that we as a company could respond to the crisis. So, when I returned to Washington, I set up *Red Cross*

Red Cross Radio Relief

Radio Relief. With the cooperation of the American Red Cross, I set up a national fundraising campaign that involved US radio stations in publicising the American Red Cross Disaster Relief telephone donation lines.

I solicited in-kind donations from a satellite company, an electronic fax transmission company and a teleconferencing company. The production staff at North American Network then contacted celebrities to record public service announcements (PSAs) containing the Red Cross's 1-800 and1-900 telephone lines. Former president Ronald Reagan and radio and TV talk show host Larry King recorded radio spots for the PSA campaign. One thousand fax notifications about the campaign and PSA broadcasts went out to radio stations.

The PSAs were broadcast by satellite, and I then arranged teleconference interviews for key American Red Cross disaster relief staff on 40 radio stations across the country. As a result of the campaign, we raised $60,000 for the American Red Cross Disaster Relief Fund.

I had by this time become skilled in using computers for a variety of purposes. I had developed two databases and written programs in the Paradox Application Language (PAL) for the company's sales and radio distribution database applications. I also developed systems for transmitting fax news releases to radio stations by integrating the company's radio database with fax communications software.

So enamoured was I with computers that I wanted to learn more. As I didn't have a computer at home, I waited until everyone had left the office and then went home to get a large bag that I could carry a monitor and computer home to study. At 11pm or so, I would return the computer to the office so no one would be aware of my secret home studies. I continued this practice for a couple of months until I could afford a computer of my own.

I developed most of the computer systems while at work in this way but also at weekends in the company office.

It was with some relief then that, in mid-1990, I installed a computer at home. The convenience of a computer at home meant that I could learn several new applications in my own time as well as explore the world of online communications. I had been attending all the computer conventions in DC during this period as well as reading the computer trade magazines. I was very aware, therefore, of current hardware and software trends.

I applied this computer knowledge in two freelance jobs, as a consultant to a special events company, and in a national hotel chain's sales department. I set up sales and accounting software for Celebrations, Inc., a special events company located in Maryland. I also trained the company owners and staff to use the software systems. In addition, I was hired to help convert an outdated computerised sales records system for the Omni Hotel in Georgetown.

Meanwhile, at North American Network, I maintained my own sales output, developing presentations to two major accounts, Andersen Windows and Toro, and I presented proposals to the client's Minneapolis-based agency, Campbell Mithun Esty. These proposals netted North American Network $140,000 in sales over two years.

During this period, I developed dozens of radio publicity proposals and met with and gave presentations to a variety of agencies, corporations, associations and government agencies. Among the most notable proposals are the ones I created for the National Alliance of Business, National Parks and Conservation Association, the European Community, and the US Food and Drug Administration.

I rewrote all the company's marketing materials during this period and developed 'How to' guides for the company's audio news release, PSA, and media tour services. I wrote, designed, and launched an audio news release handbook, *NewsFeeds Etcetera*, to the public relations community in September 1991. The handbook attracted attention from public relations practitioners. I also mailed copies to professors that taught communications at universities, knowing that some of their students would, at some future date, become company clients.

Once I had a computer at home, I learned about bulletin board systems (BBS) and dial-up systems like Minitel, a French online service that preceded the Internet. I experimented with early Internet communication protocols like Gopher, Finger, and HTML. I learned enough to say to the company that I believed that the Internet would change how we did business. What if we could distribute radio stories and soundbites via the Internet? That idea became the basis for RadioSpace, a site I developed for the company in 1994. I located an Internet provider, worked with early HTML coding tools, and launched and promoted the site to our radio station customers. One day I received a call from another Internet pioneer called Mark Cuban, who had a website called Broadcast.com. He asked if he could use our corporately sponsored soundbites on his site. We agreed, and so had a new distribution vehicle for our client stories. Broadcast.com was sold to Yahoo in 1999 for $5.7 billion, making Cuban one of the early Internet billionaires. RadioSpace was only recently retired but was used by many North American Network corporate and government clients over a 25-year period.

As I reflect on this period, my introduction to sponsored media, I see how far controlled messaging has come since those days. North American Network president leaned Republican in the 80s and 90s, not the Trumpian Republican of today, but the gentler, more societally aware Republican of the sort George Bush senior embraced. His policies supported small businesses and a belief that charities could play an important role in society. To that extent, we were apolitical, and we simply offered a voice to corporate interests that now had a way to tell their carefully crafted story, bypassing the media filters of yesterday where all news could only be heard in the 6 o'clock news reported by a trustworthy anchor newscaster. Yet those soundbites became a new form of truth even though they were sponsored by organizations that had a self-serving message. With the advent of the Internet, anyone today can be a truth-teller. Now we struggle with distinguishing the facts we need to navigate modern society vs self-serving messages, corrupt messaging or spam or disinformation that tells us that a political leader is really heading up a global network of paedophiles and that vaccines kill babies.

But then, we were building a new kind of truth machine that no longer relied on the masters of the universe. We worked with anyone that had a voice, from Kodak with its picture-taking tips to the National Rifle Association that advocated for the rights of gun owners. Drive-time radio provided the outlet. Perhaps those Kodak picture-taking tips helped capture scenes from a mass shooting.

The Media Network

In January 1991, I felt the addition of college-level training would help me satisfy my career goals as well as help sharpen my intellectual skills. While my early years in Washington DC helped me develop certain professional communications skills, I recognised the value that a college degree would give to my curriculum vitae. I was also aware that the training would provide me with many more intellectual and practical tools that I could use to help satisfy my future endeavours.

I discovered that American University offered credits toward a degree for life experience. If I could document my various life experiences in the arts, arranging publicity, putting on events, managing a team or process, I could obtain credit toward my degree. I met with an advisor and documented my decade of life experiences in the arts and music. I mapped out a curriculum in business, marketing and communications where I could write about my experience in Bristol and Hemel Hempstead managing events; in InterAction managing an arts programme. From my time at the Half Moon Theatre, I could write about arts funding. With some college credits from Bristol Polytechnic, plus my life experience, I managed to attain 30 credits towards a 120-credit degree. The rest of the credits I made up with courses in business and communications. The College-Level Examination Program (CLEP) advisor would meet with us individually and as a group to steer us on our life experience path. It was at one of these group events that I met my future wife, a petite Colombian immigrant who worked in a Latino community organization as a volunteer director. Her workplace in Adams Morgan was around the corner from where I lived and worked. Lucia had a car and offered to drive me to Adams Morgan. For years afterwards, I would explain that she offered me a ride but ended up taking me for the ride of my life!

By 1997, at 43 years old, with a degree in hand and a feeling that after ten years, I had accomplished everything at North American Network that I could, I realised that it was time to leave the company and create a business venture of my own.

It was April 21 1997 when I opened The Media Network offices at 8700 Georgia Avenue in downtown Silver Spring, Maryland, not all that far from DC. I established the firm as a sole proprietorship, with myself as President. By this time, Lucia was now my wife, and she was wholly supportive of my venture, and her position at Georgetown University allowed us to spread our income and thus cope with the initial income drop I incurred in the early years of the company. I had had over ten years of experience managing a radio consulting services business, holding senior management positions in station relations and sales, and ended that part of my career as Executive Vice President, the number two position in the company. I had managed a team of 20 full-time staff, sold to what felt like every public relations agency and trade association in the Washington DC metropolitan area, as well as many in Chicago, Los Angeles, Dallas, and other cities. I had won and managed several federal government campaign contracts, and I knew systems, from setting up a telephone system, networking computer, establishing accounting systems and setting up and using media databases. So, on that Monday, April morning, I felt at ease assembling the multiline phone system, networking computers, talking to my first client, and hiring consultant staff. I had a deadline to meet; my client wanted me to distribute a story to the top 100 radio markets the following week. In 1997, I recorded revenue of $52,457.80, expenses of $38,343.50 for a net profit of $14,132.30, not bad for a first year, but a far cry from the $3 million annual revenue in my former company.

It seemed at the time that many of the media placement companies had similar names and they all had the word network in their title: North American Network, News Broadcast Network, and now The Media Network. From my ten years' experience in radio distribution, I believed I could establish a business that could go beyond what North American Network did and leverage my knowledge of the Internet and computers to develop an efficient media distribution system that would rival other firms' capabilities. I rented an office, bought computers, networking equipment and phones, and took on two clients who needed my help placing stories on the radio. I was bringing in about $10,000 per month, which was enough to cover my office space expenses and provide a good salary.

I had two clients that starting year. One had sought me out by locating my home phone number when he learned I had left my old job. Sheldon had assembled a small public relations practice working for alternative medicine companies and knew I could get him media coverage. 1997 was the year the Fen-Phen diet pill scare happened. Fen-Phen was an anti-obesity medication marketed by American Home Products. After reports of heart disease and pulmonary hypertension, primarily in women who had been undergoing treatment with Fen-Phen, the Food and Drug Administration (FDA) requested its withdrawal from the market in September 1997. Sheldon's client wanted to take advantage of the situation by positioning their natural supplements as an effective yet safer alternative. Dr Andrew Myers was the spokesperson for the National Research Council for Health (NRCH), an organization funded by natural supplement companies. Our story pitch was, "FDA Issues Heart Disease Warning Over Popular Diet Pill Fen-Phen -- National Health Organization Urges Women to Abandon the Dangerous Diet Drug Regime for Safer Natural Alternative." Then, with that anti-Fen-Phen news hook, we were able to secure dozens of radio interviews on networks such as UPI, USA Radio Network, as well as top news-talk stations in Boston, Houston, Miami, Atlanta, Baltimore, and other markets. My client was thrilled and proceeded to send us many more radio media tour opportunities.

Meanwhile, another old client also learned I had established my own company and started sending radio news release work to me. We did a variety of stories for Pizza Hut, Bennigans Restaurants, and the J Walter Thompson agency. The pitches were harder to execute for the commercial clients, and the storyline was weak. However, the J Walter Thompson story concerned a new recruitment service designed to attract minorities to work in major corporations. The hardest sell I thought was a story for a pet food manufacturer that had, bizarrely, located a singing dog and wanted to use this as the hook to promote their product. All this just shows that in public relations, there really is a mixed bag of clients and stories. That old client of mine later asked us to establish a regular news feature for the American Heart

Association, a client and issue that was much more rewarding. We ran 18 different stories for the American Heart Association (AHA) and even established an aha@themedianetwork.com email address, a novel arrangement at the time.

1998 was a more successful year for The Media Network. We generated $172,580.81 in revenue against expenses of $125,964.66, yielding a net income of $47,132.55. I was impressed that we had managed to run a lean and profitable venture. We generated repeat business from the 1997 clients and picked up business from a long-standing PR agency, Aker Partners. I had known Colburn for several years, so I told him about my new venture. Colburn asked us to distribute stories from the US Mint, for the Van Gogh exhibition in Washington DC and for a pharmaceutical client of his.

Lucia, meanwhile, continued to work at Georgetown University as a health analyst, a position she enjoyed. The university needed help recruiting Hispanic women to its mammogram clinic in Ballston, VA. Lucia had worked with the Hispanic community for many years and had dozens of contacts in the community. Lucia also had a keen sense of what additional services would attract Hispanics to come to the clinic. Her experience and knowledge of the community and her work as a volunteer director enabled her to find bilingual staff, lay on tamales and other Latino food and provide a warm and welcoming atmosphere. Within a short period, the clinic was oversubscribed with Hispanic women eager to take advantage of a free mammogram check-up.

Children's Health – A National Media Campaign

During this period, Lucia stayed in touch with a colleague from her former position at the Delmarva Medicare Peer Review organization. Cheryl had since moved to Healthcare Finance Administration, the predecessor to the Centers for Medicare and Medicare Services. During the early Clinton Administration years, President and Hilary Clinton fought to establish a universal healthcare system. With millions of lobbying and media dollars, private industry curtailed these plans so the legislation didn't pass and would not pass until two presidents later, under Barack Obama. In 1996, with no progress on universal healthcare, the US Congress adopted a healthcare insurance system for children, the State Children Healthcare Insurance program, known as SCHIP. The SCHIP Program became the launch pad for The Media Network's work in advertising and government contracts.

Cheryl knew from Lucia that I had established a business and that I had a significant background in radio, and she asked Lucia if I would be interested in bidding for the national launch of the SCHIP program. I had written dozens of proposals to clients before, and I knew government proposals would require an extraordinary proposal effort. In 1998, I still had no full-time staff to help write the proposal. I had spent under $5,000 on contract labour that year. I knew I needed a partner to help win the bid. I had met a radio broker by phone previously and thought he might be able to help. I made a call to the Philadelphia office of Interep, looking for my contact. He was no longer there but I spent some time chatting about the project with someone named Kevin. From this chance conversation, Kevin went on to become deeply enmeshed in a project that eventually billed $2.6

million and helped launch The Media Network on a completely different path.

Kevin and I worked days and many long evenings to scour market and US census data to help to craft a proposal that we felt had a chance of winning. The target audience was households with income under $30,000 and two or more children in the household. We had a limited number of markets to propose, as the SCHIP program was supported by the states that had signed on for the program. It was obvious to me that a network advertising strategy would not work. We had to attack this on a state and market-by-market level. That spot-buy approach became our winning theme. I signed the contract, and we executed our initial buys in September and October 1998. On November 2, 1998, I sent the Department of Health and Human Services (DHHS) my first invoice for $104,120. That was by far the largest invoice I had generated for a client at any time in my career. Traditional advertising rules dictated that the agency could keep 15% of the buy as a commission while 85 percent of the invoice went towards media purchases, but the total revenue still appeared as booked revenue for The Media Network.

1998 was a good year but 1999 proved to be far better for my fledgling company. DHHS modified our contract and asked us to undertake the national launch for the SCHIP program. 1999 revenue for the SCHIP launch amounted to $1,225,346. We generated another $57,000 from our work with PR agency clients. Amazingly, I relied on contract labour to manage the national launch of the SCHIP, and so we operated with no full-time staff. I hired a receptionist and project assistant from a temp agency. Crispian became my lifeline, answering phones, ordering supplies, maintaining the QuickBooks accounting system, generating traffic instructions for radio stations, and creating colourful reports for clients. I had several media pitchers, and they also helped with radio spot production, tape duplication and the many other duties involved with mounting a national campaign.

I had put together a media strategy that would focus on getting the campaign heard on local radio stations in states that adopted the SCHIP plans. This locally focused plan won us the contract over established media entities, including ABC radio, who had presented a national plan that didn't click with the localised messaging that the Clinton healthcare team had in mind. The total contract value we had achieved for this work was about $2.5 million, quite an achievement for a small business. I had asked that the government pay us up front for the media, to which they agreed. This arrangement not only protected our cash flow, as we had to pay radio stations for airtime, but it also provided a significant float into our bank account, as we would receive the funds weeks before we had to pay stations. One Friday, I said to Lucia that we had one million dollars in the bank; what would she like to do that weekend?!

One other highlight from this period was being invited to the White House for the SCHIP launch. I had arrived early at the White House press office and the East Room where the ceremony was to take place and was asked by a staff member if we could bring copies of the radio ads that would be aired around the US. As this had not been pre-arranged, I had to place a call to my staff back at the office several miles away to ask if they could make 30 copies of cassette tapes containing the ads. Within the hour, my staff passed me a bag of cassette tapes through the White House fence, an act that today would bring a heavily armed SWAT team into view. But this was before 9/11 and the security restrictions that would follow. I dropped off the cassettes in the press room and entered the East Room for the launch ceremony. After the ceremony, we joined the rope line to meet the President and First Lady. Mrs Clinton asked what role I had played in the campaign, and I said that I was handling the radio advertising. She thanked me, and so The Media Network and over two years of hard work had landed us this ultimate accolade.

The SCHIP advertising contract allowed us to build an office infrastructure and hire a bookkeeper and project management staff, but we needed to quickly transition from this contract, which would end shortly, into a sustainable revenue stream. Building a company means finding clients that want what you offer. What I could offer was years of experience managing media campaigns, but we needed to find a niche of clients that wanted that expertise.

As a sole proprietor, I managed largely without any full-time staff. The Media Network had, since its inception, generated $1,513,645 in income and $1,240,580 in expenses for a net profit of $280,693. We had an established service base of radio advertising and media relations. Government work seemed attractive, so Lucia and I cast around for ways to tap into the federal marketplace. We had heard of the Government's minority-based 8(a) program but knew little about how to apply. As Lucia was Hispanic, we discovered that if we made some modest changes to the company structure by installing her as President, we could apply for the 8(a) program, which was designed to funnel competed and sole-source contracts to minority-owned firms. We knew we needed professional legal assistance to work through the application, so we sought out the services of a lawyer that specialized in the program. It took two attempts and over two years to be awarded the 8(a) status. Our lawyer claimed never to have lost a case. He lost ours. On March 14, 2000, we received a denial letter from the Small Business Administration (SBA) and notified our lawyer that we would resubmit the application for reconsideration on March 28. Our application was received at SBA on March 29. It was clear that we would have to make a more solid case for Lucia to be accepted as a qualifying candidate for the program. SBA denied any waiver because there was not enough evidence of substantial managerial experience during the prior two years for the 2-year waiver to apply. It took until December 2001 for our case to go through another submission as well as an appeal to the Associate General Counsel before it was finally accepted.

In September 1999, we incorporated the company, changing The Media Network to The Media Network Inc. To qualify for the 8(a) program, Lucia would have to own 51% of the business, with me as the 49% shareholder. It seemed like a fair trade, and in any case, it was obvious where our partnership strengths lay. Mine was clearly in managing a business, in public relations, sales and in systems. Lucia had a mountain of community contacts and years of experience working in community organizations. The epiphany of a social marketing company was formed slowly as we grew, adding services to our existing media relations and advertising base.

We continued to manage the SCHIP media program while meeting with other Government agencies that we believed could use our help. The niche we found was to use my marketing and media expertise coupled with Lucia's Spanish language abilities and

The Media Network trade show booth

community-based contacts to offer culturally appropriate Latino marketing, which was a growing need in the early 2000s. Forging this corporate identity meant understanding who I was so that I could build my story as I presented our capabilities to government agencies. But that identity-building exercise meant I needed to equally understand the Latino market and where the intersection would be between my media and communications expertise and the expertise that Lucia would bring from her experience.

1999 ended with a profit of $219,425. By September of 1999, it was clear The Media Network needed staff. Lucia joined the company full-time and brought with her the Georgetown University Ballston Clinic as a client, a move that brought $16,000 in revenue by the following year.

The SCHIP contract was signed by The Media Network so for it to be now signed by The Media Network Inc, it needed to be novated and agreed to by the government contracts people. The government agreed after receiving documents from the sole proprietorship and the corporation showing that management of the contract would still be undertaken with staff that had knowledge of the program and its advertising goals.

The company accountants handled the transfer of assets to the incorporated company and made book adjustments, such as writing a cheque from a sole proprietorship to Lucia for consulting work on the SCHIP program. Lucia's knowledge of research helped us do pre- and post-advertising campaign studies to test the effectiveness of the campaign.

Her contact at the National Institutes of Health Hispanic Initiative, Carlos, brought us another $50,000 for the planning of a meeting of Hispanic media. Carlos also introduced us to the National Institute on Aging where we worked on the Spanish translation of educational materials. The Health Resources and Service Administration (HRSA) hired us to do translation for the Maternal and Child Health Unit. Another Hispanic-owned 8(a) company, Lisboa, hired us to distribute television PSAs for the US Department of Energy. The Substance Abuse and Mental Health Administration (SAMHSA) hired us for radio media tours to celebrate Alcohol and Drug Recovery Month. One of the SAMHSA staff I had known from her days at the National Education Association. The NEA had hired my former company to do press work on the National Governors' Association's 1990 summit in Washington. The head of the National Governors' Association was a much-talked-about governor from Arkansas, Bill Clinton. Women.com hired us to market their website. HMA, and another Hispanic 8(a) company hired us to manage radio buys for the Centres for Disease Control and Prevention Flu campaign. And so, it was this mix of my skills in media and my contacts in Federal and public relations agencies, and Lucia's contacts in the community and in Federal agencies that we were able to build upon a three-year base of work and build out our services to include translation, focus groups and begin to form a coherent vision for The Media Network Inc.

CHAPTER 6:
IT ALL RELATES

Marriage in Heaven

t truly was a marriage made in heaven. My wife, Lucia and I were married in St Matthew's Cathedral in downtown Washington DC, the same church where President Kennedy's requiem funeral mass was held. It was summer 1993, 30 years since that 1963 date. The wedding photos could have been from

L-R Bernard, author with siblings and wedding party

Washingtonian or GQ magazine. Elegance and power couple were in the air. Our wedding reception was in the Gangplank, a waterfront restaurant in Washington DC. Yet the restaurant name might have been a metaphor for our marriage. Fifteen years later, it would all come crashing down amongst mortgage debt, bank debt, a failed marriage and a loyal husband that was so dominated by his wife that he could not stand up to her even when she demanded the impossible.

I loved being married and to an exotic wife who would take me to Colombia, to a hidden hotel spa deep in the Andes, to a pool in a country house or a finca in Tierra Caliente (hot country) where we feasted on just-plucked mangoes and oranges. We travelled over the narrow mountain road known as La Línea Andes to the one-time cocaine capital of Cali and explored Valle del Cauca, where we could pick coffee beans right off the plant. We could also chew fresh coca leaves, not that they had any effect on me. We ate freshly cooked fish served with coconut rice on San Andrés, a Colombian island off the coast of Nicaragua. Life was exotic and full of family, but after having spent so many years living a single life, I struggled to understand not only my relationship but relationships in a culture that was not my own.

Our son Dominic arrived in October 1995, just two months after my mother died. It was a confusing time of deep sadness and loss, yet of great joy at a new life and a growing family.

At the same time as growing our family, we were also growing the fledgling business, often bringing work home that we would discuss at the dinner table. This was not healthy for the marriage or our kids. As company revenues increased, my wife wanted to move to a larger house. The house we lived in cost us a little over $200,000 when we bought it in 1994. The house we ended our marriage in 15 years later cost us $1.4 million. The chasm that that cost difference made uncovered in me a range of emotions that had not surfaced before. It was a showhouse – seven bedrooms, a steam room, a huge basement, and a back garden that overlooked the suburban wilderness of the Audubon Society grounds. Wealth always made me uncomfortable. Dominic's older brother, my stepson, Andres attended Sidwell Friends School; the school was attended by children of well-to-do Washington DC residents such as the Clintons and Gores. I always felt out of place at parent-teacher events thinking that I was not worthy and certainly had no experience nor the kind of income that I assumed PTA attendee parents earned. So, to live in a house worthy of this well-appointed circle was out of character for me and made me think about our modest upbringing. Our monthly mortgage was $7,000, over three times what we were paying for our first family house. The only way around these new expenses would mean we would have to raise our salaries to $200,000 each. I managed both the household and company finances, so these considerable personal and work expenses weighed heavily on me.

Family friends were my wife's friends who were nearly always Colombian. Lucia's mother, who spoke little if any English, came to live with us and I increasingly felt marginalised, with few friends of my own and surrounded by a language and a culture that was not my own. I lacked both an understanding of the language and of how relationships worked. While I was deficient in the cultural and emotional experiences I would need for marriage survival, I did know about computers and wondered if I could apply any of that knowledge to help me understand relationships.

Understanding Relationships

So, my quest was to understand relationships, but I came to this topic with little prior knowledge. Not only did I not take the class, but it was also never offered in my world. I grew up in a boys' school, surrounded by Brothers who taught us to sing songs at Mass, and taught me French, chemistry, and Keats, but nothing about relationships. So, I started with no knowledge or even much concept about relationships. I realise that not everyone comes from such a privileged and rarefied experience, so imagine then I have landed from another planet. No, imagine I am from the planet Earth but have no navigational understanding of this subject. What I do possess is navigational knowledge on how to operate Microsoft Word, so I will use that knowledge as a foundation to understand relationships.

When others ask me how to create tables, right align a piece of text, or select an alternative word from the thesaurus, my inclination is to ask, how come they do not know about this. Before I knew Microsoft Word, years prior, I was a traveller. As a traveller, I gained insight into the basics one needs to attend to when first arriving in a new town or island. There is always a centre of town, a square. Within a short distance from this square will be a few services you will require – a bookshop, a hostel, and a place to buy food and a place to change money. Because in my youth I travelled a fair amount, I became quickly familiar with the survival and exploratory skills necessary for placing albeit a temporary footmark in town. These travel skills have come in handy outside of South America, Greece, or the Caribbean. I use them to navigate most places, just not shops. I have no navigational skills around shops. There is no ocean on the right or left of a shop, no town square, or at least none that I have any use for. I am sure today's malls were built with town squares in mind, just not me in mind, but I digress.

So, let's say over a period allowing for computers to be invented, yes, I am that old, I was able to use these travel navigational skills to find my way around a computer keyboard and a software program. These wonderful electronic tools are built around style guides, interface guides and predefined menu structures. There is architecture and a form. They all basically conform to the same set of user interface design instructions. The build kits with which software programs are made, tools like Visual Basic, software tools for the Mac, all work within the confines of conformity. In Windows programs, there is a File menu, which contains items like Save and Save As. The far-right hand menu item is Help; it is always in that position. Edit comes after File. From the Edit menu, you can cut, copy, and paste. On the Mac, the first option under the name of the program is Preferences.

In Windows programs the equivalent to Preferences is Options. Using Options or Preferences I can create my view of the world, at least my world within that program. Think of it like when you visualise a new house or new apartment – press a few buttons in the program and bingo, the bedroom is appropriately painted deep red, the kitchen yellow, and the doorbell plays U2's 'Beautiful Day'.

So how did I learn how to frame my software program world? Well, borrowing my traveller's navigational skills, I would, upon learning a new software program, scan each of the program's menu settings, as though scanning the town square looking for things like a cheap yet comfortable hotel that would benefit my short stay. In programs, I drill deeper into each menu item to find out if there are choices or program settings that offered functionality that I would need to learn more about. I would always investigate the preference pane or options selections to see how I could adjust the program to my personal style of work. Thus, my understanding of how to work that program came not so much from any innate ability but from a guided path that I practised with each new program. There was a style guide that would tell me that certain functions would always appear in a specific place. There was a scanning requirement that I had to perform to understand what all the properties and abilities of each menu dropdown would contain, and finally, there was the putting it all together, testing using whatever sample program was offered in the software, running a tutorial, or simply adding text, pictures, data of my own and pressing keys in a certain order until things made sense.

So, when I knew little about other people, I assumed each of them carried with them the same learning ability that I did about new software programs. I assumed that they would first scan the menu, investigate the options, enter test data, and let rip with the powerful functionality the software offered. My naive assumptions proved unfounded.

So, you see where this is going, or at least I hope you do. Not everyone travelled as I did, and if they did perhaps did not make the same navigational thought-leap that I took when encountering a new piece of software. Not everyone understands how software programs work. I have some abilities in that field that others do not possess. Where I fail is with cars. I have no idea where the carburettor is. I can be scammed in a heartbeat at the dealer who asks if I want to install a new manifold. Sure, what colour is it? But in the mid-years of my marriage, I also believed I failed in life because I assumed I could learn the best way to operate the relationship in the same way that I learned how to operate those software programs. I used head when I should have used heart.

My visual representation of relationships is that there is a cascading series of boxes, combinations for which must be checked off in a certain order for a particular outcome to result. I guess you could also say relationships are, to me, like a musical instrument. Certain key or string combinations will emit a certain sound. Press the wrong key combinations and it does not sound too good. My experience thus far tells me that this is also true of relationships – press the wrong button and you get an unexpected and discordant sound.

The philosophers and early mathematicians deduced through observational study that most things have patterns to them. There are seasons, heat and cold; things fall, hot air rises; numbers come in a variety of sequences; the world has a certain cadence; distant stars emit a staccato rhythm that can be picked up by high powered instruments – things like the sounds of exploding gasses or an alien language we have not yet understood. Mathematicians understand relationships between numbers. Relations are a known quantity in science, in the world. So, the sense then is that relationships being of a worldly human form should themselves have a rhythm, yet it is a rhythm and a tone that I had yet to fully understand or be in harmony with. Like random noise from space, I had yet to make sense of many of the eye movements; the short sentences meant to impart something, the hand movements, touches, changing of clothes from black to red, from red to green. I sensed each of these movements was meant to send a signal, but thus far, my detection equipment was not always powerful enough to deduce much meaning.

Thus, I must turn to my learned skills in being able to operate Microsoft Word and look for patterns of behaviours that could result in my comprehension of there being a style sheet in place, an intelligent design that I can rely on as a predictor for all future behaviour. My guess is that there are certain combinations of interaction that will, if repeated, elicit a standard response. If I say, "You look terrible," my guess, and this has not been field-tested, I should admit, is that the response would be one of anger and a verbal response which could vary from, "How dare you say that?" to "I don't care if you think I look horrible," to a fairly wide range of other possibilities depending on the sensibilities of the person being addressed.

So, here we come upon the difference between computer-to-human interaction and human-to-human interaction. The computer interaction can be predicted; a set of rules can be shaped for how the computer reacts. Press the File Save As menu and you will be presented with a location on the hard drive to save the file. The shortcut to this 'File-Save-As' process is, for those of you still following, Control S. Relationships I have noted also have some shortcuts. Crying is one that will in general, when enacted, produces a different and often speedier response that is designed by practitioners to realize a faster outcome than one of simple debate. Silences, walking away, are other shortcuts. Nonetheless, even these shortcuts do not always follow the same pattern or have the same outcomes.

As one unschooled in responding to the often-random reactions in relationships, I was looking for answers. I believed there must be a better way to navigate the highly complex system of human relationships. There did not appear to be any defining standards body that could set up a code of conduct or conduct exams. In fact, so random are relationships that there does not even appear to be consensus on right and wrong approaches. It really is a learning-on-the-job affair and so for some that come easier than for others, including me. So, I had in mind a set of recommendations that borrows the best thinking from software program designers.

First, there needed to be a common understanding around a set of design rules that would govern relationships. Without those standards, each interaction might be a series of chaotic and random behaviours. What is also missing in human relationships is a Help button. Chance upon a programming error and where does one turn? I do feel this is a design deficiency in the current human version. My guess is that with all the work in human genomes and stem cells, that Human v2.0 could be vastly improved so that it comes not only with a decent manual but some self-correcting error checks. Emit the wrong sound, words or behaviour, and the system will rapidly back play, correct the error, and allow the relationship to get back on track. Unsure of what to say in a particular circumstance? Select the Help button, set the relationship on a brief pause, and be offered a series of appropriate choices. One could also go further and have some sample relationship files preloaded, training tapes that can be played at will during downtime, and tutorials that, like some of the software language tutorials, offer praise when the correct behaviour is modelled and offer a chance to practise situations that require additional work. Options should be mandatory. Give me the ability to turn off sounds I don't like and pre-set borders that work for me. Version 2.0 also can cut behaviour that does not work, copy that which does, and paste good ideas from one set of relationships into another set of relationships. So Cut, Copy, and Paste in relationships instead of just Cut and Run; a Save Relationship button, a better Word? On later reflection, this analogy suffers from being a single point of view. In relationships, there are two parties, two menus, two buttons and an endless combination of outcomes.

With these random thoughts, a deteriorating marriage, and a belief that I was an alien in my own house, I retreated from our home in Chevy Chase, Maryland to the West Virginia countryside. It was 2007, I was now 53 years old, and it was my birthday. Berkeley Springs is a place of healing, a town resplendent in spas, reiki, and yoga practices. As I reflected after a day of walking and healing, I wrote the following words to my wife.

Berkeley Springs

This evening is my last in Berkeley Springs and you are probably wondering what I have learned. You said yesterday evening on the phone that it sounded like I had gone on a vacation. That hurt me because what I have experienced these past days has been anything but. During these past few days, I have examined every aspect of my life; I have pored through every emotion. I have prayed to my mother, my grandmother, Brother Joseph, Brother Henry, every teacher and guide I ever had. I feel like I have been living in the movie It's a Wonderful Life except I have wondered which life, and which wonder?

I have stared down the highway into the headlights of oncoming 18-wheelers and wondered how fast I could make the pain go away. I have experienced loneliness. I also have a deeper affection for West Virginians and thank them for the kindness they extended to me these past days. I am grateful to the postal worker who so graciously helped me mail Christmas packages to Dominic's cousins when I could barely speak because of my heavy cold. She made my day with her smiling face and her helpful gestures. I wonder how much I too could make a difference in someone's life; make their day if I should extend the same kindness and help.

I wrote that these days had been a gift. I have gone thru every range of emotion you can think of but when I opened your birthday gifts, and for many hours before, one prevailing emotion came through. I recall the times we sat with Amma, the intuit teacher we engaged to help our marriage. She showed us pictures of how if you write the word love on a glass of water and it freezes, the ice crystals are better formed than if you had written hate. I called your mother from a mountaintop, and she was warm and loving and gracious, and I thank her for that. She is my mother here on earth, you said that once. I called Dominic every morning to wake him for school. He knew that even though he never answered the phone. He knew I was there for him.

I have no answers; I came here looking for guidance. I called out to my mother, but I guess I either never called hard enough or she never heard me. I was told that if I asked her to come to me in my sleep, give me a message while I was dreaming but ask her to have me remember her message when I woke, that I would, it would have happened. I did not hear her message though. But perhaps I did feel her love. Perhaps that is what this test has been all about.

I came to West Virginia in search of something, in search of self. I found a heart. I found a pain that I did not drown with drink. I investigated the pain. I investigated the hurt. I dwelled on every moment that this gift of time has given me. I have passed through life running on cruise control, unaware of the life passing me by. I have held tight to my emotions for fear of what they might unleash. But by holding onto my feelings, my emotions, I unleashed another journey that was this: a journey into my soul, who I am, what I value, what I believe, what I dream. I am not finished. Berkeley Springs was only the beginning and whatever may come of it, I thank you for your love. I thank you for your wisdom, your vision, your affection, and the family I have now.

I am thankful for this time, for you, for our family. I am grateful for a life I often feel I do not deserve and do not understand. I have so often retreated when I should have advanced. That has been my weakness from the time, as a child, I never completed swimming the whole length of the swimming bath and I gave up at the three-quarter mark. So often I have tried but could not lift my weight to make ten push-ups. Today I did twelve and could have made fifteen, but I had just showered and felt I should not get too sweaty.

I have missed much of life, but I believe I have an inner core. I have still much to learn, and I must learn to savour moments in favour of solving problems and weaving a careful strategy. I must learn to first recognize my feelings, express them as emotions and communicate with my heart more than my head. Amma's words, that I will do much more in my life to come with my heart than my head, still rings in my mind.

I do not know what the future brings. If I have lost a life, I am truly destitute and do not know which way to turn. I do know that whatever I may have lost I have gained wisdom, a wisdom that I could not have gained in any other way. I feel like I am in a life game where I am being tested to see what I am truly worth. The value I am being asked for is a value that I alone can place.

The value I place on my life I can only measure in the value I place on you, my son Dominic, my stepson Andres, and your mother. You have been and still are such a huge, massively important, and very close part of my life, and I am grateful for all you have given me over these years. These things I can see clearly.

I am no longer clear about what value my career holds, as my career and our lives have become so intertwined. I know my value but where it should lie is a mystery to me. Things may be clear in a year or so. Who knows how long it will take for me to unpick the last decade, the last twenty years, all my years in this country? None of that is clear to me. I must do some more soul-searching there.

So, what did West Virginia do for me? It taught me about life, some parts of life, not all of life. I walked along an old rail-to-trail track. I found it off the road to Hancock, which, by the way, has just one traffic light in the whole of the town. The trail was straight as train tracks are. I could make out some dark shapes in the distance and by the number of cars in the car park, I assumed the shapes might be people. I would have been grateful for the company, so I walked toward them. The shapes never moved, so next, I thought they were dogs. I have been afraid of dogs since I was five and was bitten by one. The shapes never barked. Next, as I walked closer to the dark shapes, I thought they may be bridge trusses. A bridge would have been good along an otherwise uneventful path. And so, I kept on walking on this cloudy overcast day, yet the shapes turned out to be of little consequence even as I passed them. I could not tell you what they were. They were as mirages in my mind, a placeholder for the long path, a goal I could strive to reach, yet they never in fact appeared like any solid thing, like I was chasing the end of the rainbow.

But from my rail-to-trails walk, I experienced a journey. I am an adult. I am supposed to know what I want and where I want to go. But the truth is, if life is a journey there is no way to go – it is the journey itself that is the learning experience, the destination as it were.

So where have I been to these past few days? I have been on a journey that taught me about emotions, family, and something of love. But this journey is not ended yet and while I see the clock closing on midnight and I must end this piece of writing now, I realise all too well that my journey is only beginning.

Your loving husband, Steve

Separation

2008 was a strange year for Dominic and me. Lucia, my wife of 15 years, and I separated in April that year. The Media Network Inc. at that time was generating some $4.5 million in annual sales and had a good backlog of work. Yet a rupture in my marriage sadly was also a rupture in my business relationship with The Media Network Inc. Through mediation and later divorce, we divided our assets, including my interest in the company. My wife asked me to leave the business I founded.

I rented a house not far from the family home. I was unemployed for several months. During that time, I realised I had never interviewed for a job in the US, and I had been there for over 20 years! In September 2008, I landed a senior-level marketing position with a consulting firm. The firm had previously tried to acquire a financial stake in our firm in a bid to maintain a connection to a minority-owned business that could feed it government contracts. The firm offered me a corner office and a high-end Mac computer. They agreed to my proposed title of VP of Digital Strategy and Innovation. As social media firms such as Twitter and Facebook had built their powerful platforms, my job was to help guide the company in leveraging social media to benefit its public health campaign contracts.

In the period between separation and the job, I did a top-to-toe audit of myself, undertaking a wide range of professional and career development courses. I shared myself with large and small groups of people, and for a reticent Englishman, that was a top-to-toe change indeed. I did intensive weekend training in a men's group (or was it a mend group?) designed to both freeze and starve you to death while fixating on developing a life mission. I meditated in circles, danced in drum circles, and joined the neighbourhood community, starting with a tour of neighbours' gardens, a tortuous event but one that made me a new set of friends. I came almost first place in a divorced and separated group melon seed spitting competition (yup, you did need to read that twice, didn't you?), did Myers Briggs, the well-known career test, and learned I was slightly extrovert, not the introvert I had taught myself I always was. I did weekend courses on empathy while feeling I really needed just sympathy. Amongst all these activities, I also did a course in intensive Spanish conversation. Throughout this long retreat, I somehow advanced.

I recall one professional development event where I went to the registration table and I said, "Look, my life has just collapsed – I have lost my marriage, my business, my family, my friends and my house, what can you do for me?" Perhaps I had expected a concrete response like, "The special for the day is lamb cutlet, will that do?" but instead they said, "That's OK, you are in the right place!" I had supposed I must have reached the pearly gates because, in my forsaken state, there was nowhere else for me to be. I stood in front of the stage microphone at one development course and became myself, told the audience my story and, in so doing, inspired others. I found a mission: "To be authentic and passionate about life and act with integrity, courage, and power to inspire others."

I found the possibility of a new life, a life that belongs to me; has always belonged to me. I lost a marriage, a family life, a luxurious house, and a successful business, but through it all, I found myself, I found my heart. I battled an army of voices that sapped my confidence. I wrote a good deal during my period of sojourn. As I wrote, my spell checker made me realise that understood and undersold are easily confused. I learned that I could communicate using powerful, simple words.

My relationship with my son Dominic by that time had never been stronger. We laughed, joked, and shared so many interests, and I thanked him for keeping me young, turning me on to new music, and helping me rediscover the child in myself. I had by then a three-bedroom house about a quarter of the size of the family home I once had. I had a job I enjoyed, and a multitude of new friends but also a void that cannot be replaced – only a period of life that I can learn from.

It was April 2008, and it was my last night in Flushing Meadow, the family home. It was a poignant and very heavy-hearted time. My losses seemed incalculable – my marriage of 15 years, the family unit that I loved, my family home with all its splendour, spaciousness, colour and comfort, my business and a decade of work, the parties we had, my daily walks to the school bus stop with Dominic, Bentley, the dog, trips to Colombia, my friendship with Lucia's Colombian family, and if we sold the house, a lifetime of savings.

My new home was in Silver Spring, Maryland. I had all the utilities switched on, and Internet and cable installed. I moved mine and Dominic's bed there with the rest of my clothes and personal belongings and a desk for Dominic. I had taken a few mementoes, just small things like the Chinese embroidered cloth my sister Clare gave me, the sangria pot and cups Sean bought for our wedding, the pottery piece Bernard gave us for our wedding, the elegant, boxed cutlery set that Dad, Mum and Auntie Maureen gave us for our wedding. I knew I must build a new life and I started that with a trip to a life skills event held by The Landmark Forum, an intensive workshop on life's possibilities.

I was not planning to rebuild my life at this stage, and I could feel a hole in my heart and deep pain at all that I had lost, but I vowed to move on. I thought then that it would take me years to understand what had happened. So much was thrown away, or perhaps just recycled for another life ahead. Here in this new house was great sadness and painful memories of a life that was now behind me. A new life awaited me and while I carried deep pain, I knew I had much to offer and I could hold on to the idea that this loss, this pain, was meant to be, a life lesson, a life toning for the path ahead.

Something in Common

I completed one of the personal development courses on a Sunday evening and felt mentally refreshed, though perhaps not yet transformed as the course leader would have us be. Still, I felt good about the world, though perhaps not good about myself. I had no money, and I was reflecting upon my poverty as I entered the 7-11 at 1 am that Monday morning. I needed bread, figuratively and by way of food. Bread is a staple and comfort food for me. Mixed with butter and marmalade, I could be transported back to my humble beginnings. Bread is cheap or so I thought.

As I entered the store a panhandler caught my attention and asked for money. I had just signed up for unemployment assistance and was not feeling particularly flush, but I was feeling good-hearted. I scoured the store shelves for nutritious but cheap bread. My pre-sliced brown loaf came to $3.50, an outrageous fortune I thought. I had expected $2.00 or so, perhaps something that has not been seen since wartime. I had never paid attention to food prices before now. When your household income is $400,000 a year you don't pay much attention to the cost of a loaf of bread.

For the past several days at the development course, I had been sharing my story of riches to rags, my separation, and my job hunt with fellow course participants. My story was ingrained in my head, and I felt inclined to ask the panhandler for his story. I handed him a dollar bill and sat down next to him. It is 1:15 am. I asked, "What's your story?"

He said he was from Newport News, Virginia. He pulled out his driver's license as though to offer proof. At this point, I am thinking to myself, I have nothing, you have nothing, we have something in common. He proceeded to tell me he had separated from his wife, yeah, we really did have something in common. I almost drew my hand upward as though to give him a high five, but somehow his melancholy did not seem suited to hand gestures like that. He needed $36.50 for a bus ticket to get back to Newport News. I suggested a place where he might find day labour opportunities. He knew the place. We spent a few moments together, me thinking about my impoverished self, and he too, two souls in the night, on different life paths which just happened to coincide on a warm summer night.

A couple of customers approached the store, and he turned his attention away from me and back to his real job of asking for money. Our brief connection was over, and I returned to my car and to my home, thinking that I had gone into the 7-11 poor but had exited richer, richer for the experience of learning about someone with whom I shared a common thread of life. Yet I also thought my panhandler acquaintance had not been born homeless; he did not exit his mother's womb homeless. I had spent the last 3 days on a course about creating my life's possibilities, yet here I was talking to someone to whom life had happened to them. My education, my upbringing, and my life experience gave me the chance to rebuild my life from the ashes of a failed marriage. But what possibilities lay ahead for him? I returned to the comfort of my rental home to try and find answers.

CHAPTER 7:
LEARNING FROM LIFE

Passion

So, here's the thing – if you don't have it, you are not human. Everyone has it. I am talking about passion. Some people have a passion for sports. I don't. When someone says in the lunchroom, "Are you watching the game tonight?" I panic. What game? Card game, game show, or the game with a ball? Which ball, the small one, the big bouncy one, or the oval one? I have no idea what people mean when they talk about the Wizards, the Rockets, the Weenies or whatever these teams are called. None of these sports calls to me.

Some people love gardening – they will spend all day in their back yard, fiddling with tools, grasses, turf and seedlings. My sister will spend hours in the garden weeding, trimming her bush so to speak. She takes after my late father who had a prize English country garden complete with a splendid display of roses, a rash of the colour purple, orange and yellow, a colourful turn of phrase for plants I no longer know the name of. That used to be me 30 years ago, but not now. I would often turn sod, tussle with turf, and tweak mother nature to produce a flatter lawn or a rocky outpost of flora and fauna. I now live in a rental house, complete with a garden, but it is not mine. Not having a yard of my own anymore sort of sucked that gardening passion out of me.

Take writing – because while I love to write, when I must write, I don't like it. It feels like a duty, one more thing that prevents me from just hanging around, fiddling with the computer, getting lost in the mindless task of getting the PlayStation to talk to my Mac.

Today I watched a YouTube video from Shekhar Kapur, a Bollywood director obviously of some repute speaking about storytelling at TED, a conference about technology, entertainment and design, new age for new thinkers. He spent 20 minutes telling an enraptured audience in India that the way he approaches storytelling is to first panic. Like meditation he said, panic flushes the mind, a thought that sets off the notion of a sudden but ultimately refreshing colon cleanse. As I listened to Shekhar, his panic notion, the rapid cleanse is an opportunity for new ideas to fill a vacuum. So, I passed on gardening as a passion, but I did take up meditation as a practice, mostly to calm a frenetic mind from the hazards of working with my wife. Imagine that I married a hot-blooded petite Latin woman, and we were married to the job, the small marketing agency business we ran together. There was no escape, no cave that this man from Mars could hide in. Life, money, profession, career, daily tasks were all mixed up in a cauldron mired in fiery sauces of opposing forces; she a Latin, me an Englishman with the genes of a Presbyterian Scot. This was not an ethnic coupling that blended easily in life. I hated my existence, but I was trapped in a marriage and a business.

My wife said I needed to find my passion, so I looked for it on Amazon. Amazon had several good books including one I bought that came with a workbook. Great, I could spend time drilling through a passion audit, whittle down my interests until I could finally lock onto something that I could pass off as a passion. The Amazon passion scheme timed out. I found the task of working

CHAPTER 7: LEARNING FROM LIFE | PASSION

through the book tedious and yet passion, I assumed, is not supposed to be tedious.

Separation from my wife of fifteen years was anything but tedious. She asked me to leave the house and the marriage, and I did so among considerable drama. I had always thought that I would experience one moment in life that would cause me to shift my view of the world. I thought that one day while visiting Colombia I might be kidnapped by guerrillas and must live off leaves and insects in the jungle. That would have taught me a lasting life's lesson. No longer would I idly shop on Amazon looking for my passion. Life itself would be a passion because I would have seen life pass by me as the guerrilla put a gun to my head in one last attempt to extract my family fortune as ransom money. But Bogota is not like that, so I came home on the plane passionless once more. Instead, my gun to the head was divorce.

The solitude of singleness was not conducive to finding one's passion, so I took up dancing. I was a well-built, slightly stocky male in his mid-fifties, so this was an unusual step. Nonetheless, I arrived at the dance studio to find myself surrounded one weekday lunchtime by lithe young lawyers in leotards, themselves all presumably escaping the office for a moment of moving passion. This was an opportunity to move briskly or slowly around the room, finding one's level while taking on the appearance of a tree. This was dance improvisation, and it was the improvisation part that provided some escape for me – anything goes in improv, even stocky middle-aged males. We all have a place and dance, and movement is simply an interpretation of whatever we want it to be. Dance was liberating, reminding me of my younger days in the theatre. It was liberating at least until the 21-year-old ballet dancer and the circus-trained acrobat joined the dance group, each appearing as graceful artists set off against the background of portly pretentiousness that was me. I gracefully stepped aside from the dance troupe realizing that the physical arts were not my passion, my calling, nor anybody else's call to me.

Music might be magic, I thought. I had been invited to play the harmonica during some of the dance sequences. While I have been playing the harmonica for 30 years, I had never played in public. I had played alone to a record player, finding a beat and a rhythm among the private notes. I considered myself good but playing in public to an audience would be the real test. Because this was improv, I could have burped and made an impression, so making tuneful harmonic burps was all I was tasked to do. I passed that test, and so felt some confidence that music might be a passion. I attended a jam session in someone's home, strangers with guitars. A friend had invited me. I wailed away feeling quite good that to me at least the noises emanating from my instrument had some sort of tune. I landed a date out of that event, so with supreme confidence, I invited her to a blues concert at a local bar. Wow, I could pass myself off as a musician keeping up with the scene. As we sat there soaking up the music, I was simply experiencing another journey on the way to finding passion, but I realised that not everyone is on that journey – my date was not on that journey. Nonetheless, I longed for a creative spark between us. She said she loved to write. I thought, whoopee, we can exchange short stories and critique one another's work. As we delved into each other's lives I learned she loved to write reports. We ended our journey a week later.

My passion is not dating or music but it may be. I do love to create, whether it is a piece of writing or some marketing innovation. I love people and would rather converse than work, feeling I am inventing, creating something through my words, and I am. I am creating relationships as I meet people. Even via a failed date, I am creating a thought about what I am not and how I should spend my time. So, I go through life envious of those who know their place, who have divined their passion from an early age. They will go far because they will enter their young career full of enthusiasm to continue what they know and love, whether it is computers, writing reports or gardening. They will pursue their lot in life, and I will pursue mine. They will have fulfilled a life mission and attained a great achievement. They will have setbacks as I have done. They will have journeyed as I have done. Perhaps their goals are the destination – a fulfilment of their passion, the ultimate moment, the moments in music or movement that I do not seek. Instead, I will enjoy the scenery because life is the same, only the scenery changes like a theatre set. For me there is no end, no destination. I have moments of truth, but my passion is the journey, the many moments, the many people, the richness that is life. I have no passion, I am no longer wedded to a single thing, even a single person. The journey is everything, the moments fuel my exuberance. I realize my renaissance. My passion is life.

Selling Health

I fell into public health by accident. I described earlier how The Media Network had come into being and had initially just been my venture. Lucia had admired what I had been doing and wanted to find a way that she could help the business. She had no media or business experience, but she did know a lot of people, one of whom asked if I would be interested in bidding on a large advertising project out of the White House, which was how we had got involved with generating airings on radio stations for the launch of the State Children's Health Insurance Program (SCHIP). That assignment helped me to understand private employer-sponsored and public health insurance in the form of Medicare and Medicaid, insurance programs for seniors and people with limited income. Our Latino marketing contracts for the National Highway Safety Administration and Centers for Medicare and Medicaid Administration helped me understand the challenges immigrant communities have navigating and paying for public health in the US. Many Latinos were fearful of enrolling in public health programs or even enlisting with a family physician for fear their names would be given to the immigration authorities. When some years later, I joined WebMD, the well-known US health information website, I became attuned to the stark differences between the budgets of pharmaceutical-backed health campaigns versus those undertaken by US Government agencies.

I was responsible for several health campaigns in The Media Network, including managing the marketing for a contract with the Substance Abuse and Mental Health Services Administration. In 2010 opioid abuse was just beginning to hit the news headlines. Purdue Pharma began aggressively marketing Oxycontin in 1995 as a safer and less addictive pain killer. Pain meds were prescribed for every type of pain or injury, but the drugs were highly addictive and were causing over 100 deaths daily. I was working at the consulting firm when the National Institute on Drug Abuse (NIDA) issued a request for a proposal to develop training for physicians to screen for opioid abuse. Coincidently, I received a LinkedIn request to connect from someone at WebMD that offered physician training. Together, the two companies, the consulting firm and WebMD developed a response to the NIDA proposal. Our response was successful, and we were awarded a $900,000 contract. The resulting education curriculum attracted over 200,000 physicians and became an oft-cited success in WebMD's portfolio. Shortly after the award, in 2011, WebMD asked me if I was interested in joining their newly-created government contracts acquisition team, which was later rebranded as Public Health Solutions. Our mission was to leverage the large 70 million consumer visitor audience that WebMD had, coupled with their two million physicians and healthcare provider membership that its sister site, Medscape, had, and so develop health campaigns and healthcare provider training solutions for the Federal Government.

Much of WebMD's corporate appeal was designed to attract private sector clients. We were the number one health information website, often a target of memes and jokes in late-night talk shows and social media, as everyone knew that they could check their minor symptoms and come away with the idea that they had a terminal illness. Still, the website had great appeal to Federal agencies that wanted to reach both providers and consumers.

I recreated marketing materials specific for government agencies, stripping out corporate-speak such as "competitive blunting" in favor of language that spoke about behavior change, the much sought-after result for any public health program. After all, if through awareness campaigns you could direct pain sufferers to safer treatment than opioids or encourage parents of pre-teens to get the HPV vaccine that prevents cancer, we could improve health and change people's behaviours. Training providers on preventing infections at a time when Ebola was a concern or helping guide providers on screening for substance use disorder or even seniors' ability to drive safely were all of interest to the Federal Government. I spent over ten years presenting WebMD's capabilities to dozens of Federal agencies, attracting over $28 million in contract dollars. And I sweated every dollar.

The government does not act quickly and has mountains of rules for whom it should work with and how. I knew how to position the company to be not only attractive to the government but compliant with all its rules. I distilled and adapted dozens of slide decks, offering a dizzying amount of promotional and educational products into a streamlined offering that offered health provider education, campaign materials dissemination, and health provider surveys that could offer Federal health agencies insights into provider practices. Over the decade and more I worked at WebMD, we generated millions of media impressions, millions of provider learner sessions, and thousands of completed surveys leading to insights that would help guide government health policies.

Dealing with government bureaucracy has never been my interest nor strength and during the times I got frustrated by the system, I would call upon the memory of my nurse mother, who spent years taking care of hospital patients and our family. While times had changed and my role was not in direct patient care, I could direct my energies toward the same caring for others ability that my mother had undertaken for so many years. That sense that I was carrying forward a maternally guided motivation helped me through so many days when I faced contract roadblocks or when management pushed me for end-of-quarter sales numbers when I knew I could not deliver the same dollar volume as my pharmaceutical sales colleagues who would often deliver sales results in the many millions of dollars. Pharma is much more active and has greater investments in making their products successful than has the government in combating messaging in health.

Perhaps the ultimate test of my ability to extract dollars from the government was just as the Covid pandemic began and a nationwide and global lockdown ensued. Sales are driven through interpersonal connections, which involve meeting with agencies face to face, at appointments, and at conferences. I used to travel several times a year to Atlanta to visit the Centres for Disease Control and Prevention (CDC), to Boston, San Francisco, Denver, Orlando, Chicago, and many other cities. As the world shut down, those face-to-face opportunities vanished, to be replaced by on-camera Zoom and Google Meet meetings. Conferences provided a way to talk to Government officials, who, when away from the formality of their office would speak more freely about their needs. Now those serendipitous meetings at the buffet line or bar were no more. Instead, we were all the same two-dimensional picture and voice, absent of any detectable body language that might indicate interest or empathy.

Yet here we were, the top health website for providers and consumers, there must be something we could do to help combat Covid. I researched a list of all the principal staff at health agencies and started selectively calling staff to offer our services. Out of a list of several hundred people, I found a physician in the Office of the Assistant Secretary for Preparedness and Response (ASPR) that had an interest in us developing training videos on telehealth. That conversation turned into a large contract and gave me the confidence that sales were possible during Covid. But the public health landscape had changed dramatically because of Covid. The sales environment had changed, and the fun of travel had ended suddenly. I was 66 years old, and it was time for a change.

At the end of 2020 I decided to semi-retire and work part-time for WebMD, keeping my sales hat in the ring and preserving some elements of professional status. Management agreed to me hiring an account manager partner who could take care of the day-to-day contract and reporting needs, allowing me to focus during my half-time on sales. My previous boss at the radio firm learnt that I was semi-retired and offered me a consultant position advising the company that I had worked for 25 years ago on marketing. The free time that my new status offered has provided me with the space to reflect on my career and so draw some conclusions and insights.

Life's Lessons

As we begin a new year in 2022, with over two years of the pandemic behind us and an uncertain future, my thoughts turn to the 20 or 25 years I may have left in life and what I have learned over the past decades of work. The political landscape in the US has changed ever since Donald Trump became president. While he is no longer in office, he maintains a very strong grip on the Republican party, which has since passed numerous laws that will make it harder to vote in future elections. The demographics of the US have become more diverse, more multicultural, traits that favour Democrats over Republicans. For Republicans to maintain power, they need to select the voters that will vote Republican, disenfranchising Democratic voters through changed voting district maps, voter ID laws, and regulations that make it difficult for blacks, Hispanics and poor people to vote. These voting changes will move the US to more of a single party-political system and, should Trump once again win the Presidency, an authoritarian, dictatorial system of government.

At the same time as we face elements of fascism, the world is facing a fast-changing climate that provides tinder for fires in the West and flooding everywhere. I wonder where I can live safely for the remainder of my life to escape fires, floods... and fascism. Many people around the world are having the same idea. We are living in a vastly changed world; one that changed in March 2020 at the start of the new decade with the Covid pandemic and one that changed in 2016 with the election of Donald Trump and the British people's decision to exit the European Union. On February 24 2022, Russia invaded Ukraine, and so began a new and dangerous Cold War where Russia has been economically ostracized, and Russian President Vladimir Putin is threatening nuclear war. It seems that all that we knew, all that provided us with climate and political stability, is fading fast. Where do we go from here? In an uncertain world, all I can do is reflect on what I have experienced in life in the hope that there is an answer.

What have I learned? I have condensed ideas from each stage of my life, noting what I have might carry forward.

Of religion, it was not religion that caused me to spend five years of my early life in a religious institution. I made that pre-pubescent move in 1968 out of a spirit of adventure mixed with some romantic ideas about missionary life, albeit one that I would undertake in rural Berkshire, not the Borneo jungle! My early morning rosary walks around the school's grounds became less of a calling to God or Our Lady and more of an appreciation of the nature which surrounded me, the woodland walks, the bees that Brother Henry kept and the solitude of a young boy finding his way in life unobstructed from the all-encompassing technology we endure today. So, through nature, through solitude, I can now value my own company, and the pleasure of everyday walks in nature.

Of relationships, I learned to be true to myself, to voice my concerns, and speak out when things don't feel right. I am now aware that projected feelings that often come as accusations, these are not about me but about the other person's feelings and hang-ups. Today, while I still make mistakes, I trust my gut and don't try to be a people pleaser. I know now that it neither helps myself or my partner because I am hiding what I really feel and that helps no one.

Of the arts and theatre, and indeed much of my professional life in communications, I learned that great art happens when you have a visionary creative director coupled with an equally strong administrator – the creative director inspires, bringing creativity to life, while the administrator makes sure it is all done within budget. You need both an ideas person and a strong production team that can deliver on that vision, that creativity. Culture is fundamental to human existence, so if we can touch people in ways that resonate with their daily lives yet still explain a point of view, can we broaden our appeal? In a sales environment, you need not only a salesperson who can excite clients with a vision of what they will achieve with your product or service, but you need a strong delivery person or team to bring that vision to its final execution.

There are genuine fears about the new world of technology. We all rushed headlong into the brave new world and embraced all the shiny new toys and experiences without fully understanding how this would fundamentally change our lives, changing forever how we interact with others. Yet the technology machine is in constant motion, always changing, with operating system updates, venture capital-backed new services, 5G networks, and yes, lifesaving vaccines. I believe in vaccines' lifesaving properties, but that doesn't mean that I don't have misgivings about the power of pharmaceutical companies and their constant search for treatments for ailments that we didn't even know we had. In the US, there is light regulation of supplements and medical devices. I made a point of embracing technology early on because I knew it would change so much about our lives and I wanted to understand. However, if I were to lump the totality of all these confusing and fast-moving changes together, I, too, now have misgivings about technology and its misuse. Yet, we all know the value where technology does bring us together.

In 1991, we had a family trip from the UK to Florida, and I talked about this wonderful new world of computers to my father, who at that time was 64 and had a BBC computer at home, a poor substitute for the advanced machines we have today. He was keen to know something of what I knew, so we rented a computer, and I taught him how to use CompuServe, an early email system. When we returned home, he experimented more with CompuServe and he credited our time together in Florida with helping him embrace technology. At 94 years old, he regularly used Facetime, Alexa, Quicken, his iPad, and his iPhone.

But not everyone has the patience or desire to spend hours testing the latest software as I did. We all expect technology to work as simply as turning on a light or tap/faucet. But software and technology today are so complex yet so interdependent on those that use it that we get frustrated when it doesn't work as expected. This lack of understanding of technology, including lifesaving vaccines, has been easily exploited with simplistic and devious messages allowing conspiracy theories to flourish and far-right dictatorial forces to manipulate people's emotions.

Is there still an opportunity to slow down the clock of technological advances to allow us all to take a breather and catch up? Perhaps not, but meanwhile, schools, community centres, and civil organizations perhaps should be helped with financial backing to help explain and put in a wider context the rapid changes we see today. Is empathy around these rapid changes still possible?

The divisions we see today were there in the 1980s, as I saw in attempting to raise funds for the theatre from the London Dockland Development community and the trade unions. The divisions have only grown sharper and more violent, but they were always there. I attempted to bridge a divide, perhaps naively, in the Half Moon fundraising by appealing both to the trade unions and the property developers, both of whom had vastly different missions.

In the pre-digital era, when I entered the world of arts and entertainment, we publicized events by pasting posters and flyers on construction site walls, near tube stations and in other public places in an illegal tradition known as fly posting. We would pay students to post the flyers in all the main student areas of town. Today we use social media to achieve the same purpose, but we have more control around who sees our message. We can target audiences by interest, geo location, or by association with similar events. We can instantly share our interest and buy tickets at the same location where we saw the publicity. And we can perform these tasks while saving trees because all communications are now electronic.

But where we might save trees, our ability to call up any song, any film, any book or article is supplanted by our equal ability to order physical products wrapped tightly in plastic and cardboard for receipt in hours or the next day. The packaging contributes to massive waste and its transportation using fossil-fuelled vehicles brings us closer to a climate calamity. Our 21st-century challenges now seem epochal, world-changing events that could lead to societal breakdown or human extinction, not merely a change in government.

The Internet was supposed to bring us all together as the mass communications capability would drive greater human understanding. This may have been true in Iran in 2009 during the green revolution or Egypt in 2010 as the Internet played a major role in citizens being able to share information about protests. "Where activists were once defined by their causes, they are now defined by their tools," Malcolm Gladwell writes in *The New Yorker*[1], attributing online activism for grassroots action. In the same 2010 article Mark Pfeifle, a former national-security adviser, later wrote, calling for Twitter to be nominated for the Nobel Peace Prize. Yet a decade later the same social media channels have instead been used to spread disinformation. Tools that we heralded as being our saviour are now part of our societal destruction. And Twitter has now been acquired by the richest person in the world, Elon Musk, which is hardly a portend for fair balance.

In 1984, during a short stay in Washington DC, I visited the Pentagon and bought a copy of the book *Spycatcher* by Peter Wright, the former assistant director of MI5. The book was banned in Britain because the Tory government believed it compromised policy decisions. Yet here in America, the book was available for sale. I could also pick up a copy of the US Department of Defense budget in the same bookshop. I marveled at how open and transparent the US was compared to the very closeted secretive Britain. Yet a generation later, in 2022, Republicans are now banning books about race relations and transgender issues. In 2015, the US Supreme Court ruled in favor of gay marriage, yet just 7 years later Florida lawmakers want to ban discussions of sexual orientation and gender identity in schools under a

---

[1]   https://www.newyorker.com/magazine/2010/10/04/small-change-malcolm-gladwell

bill known as the *Don't Say Gay* Bill[2]. Voter repression laws that Republican-led states are now passing because of Donald Trump losing the 2020 election go against all the civil rights work of the 1970s and 80s. And so, in a final death knell to reproductive rights and women's control over their own bodies, the Supreme Court has overturned Roe vs Wade, the landmark 1973 Supreme Court decision that protected a woman's right to choose. This stuttered, go forward then backward approach to history deadens our spirit to keep advancing human rights. Instead, technology and its manipulators scheme to overturn our social advances. We must push the rock of human rights back up the hill again.

So, where do I find myself in the early years of the 2020s? I've covered events in my life in this book stretching back across seven decades – my early life in religion, searching for answers from a higher spirit; my humanistic endeavours in hospitals and care homes; my fun, creative days in music and the theatre; my experiences of new and diverse cultures through travel; my marriage, and my decades of work in communications and in public health. It's been a long and varied journey, from 1950s' Sheffield, England, to 2020s' Maryland, US. It's one that has provided few clear answers, at least to me, but hopefully has raised some reflections, questions, and provocations about the journey the world has taken during these turbulent decades.

Where would I have been today had I stayed in England? I wonder if I might have followed one of my St Cassian's juniorate classmates whom I learned had slipped away into alcoholism. What career post theatre would I have embraced among savage cuts in the arts? I could only conjecture what might have happened had I not taken the plane to Brazil and stayed instead in London.

---

2   https://www.flsenate.gov/Session/Bill/2022/1557/BillText/Filed/PDF

For all the advances shown in communications, technology, and the general health and wealth of the developed world, sadly, it feels like it is all culminating right now in the most challenging epoch the world has known. But at least I feel as if I have some experience and perspective with which to face it all.

As a Christian Brother in training, a mini-monk, I never made it to taking vows or donning a black habit. Instead, I ventured into the world of rock and roll and punk – Monk to Punk, so to speak. That wild transition set the course for a no-holds-barred approach to my career. I could experiment, take on a challenge, and even change the scenery, as I did with my trip to Brazil and my emigration to the US. My decade working in England during the 1970s and '80s opened the creative world for me, yet I was a manager of events rather than a creator or performer at those events. I produced rock concerts and festivals, I managed theatre companies, and I raised money to build a theatre, but I never wrote a play or played in a band. I've been involved in communications but have rarely been in front of the microphone myself. I've been an advocate at the highest level for improved public health but am no physician. I've been an enabler, a director, and a catalyst rather than a front-line performer. Does that diminish what I have done and have achieved? Objectively, not at all, but as I have written out these distinctions, I have revealed a latent need to perform and to create, to display talents in a direct and upfront way. But it's never too late to develop those abilities and form those experiences, and in recent years, I've taken a few steps to do so. I have played the harmonica on a soul album,[3] performed with a band[4] in a play and was a cast extra in a couple of short films. Today, I play harmonica in a rock and roll band with a top Nashville guitarist, and I have teamed with another musician to

---

3   Songs for Janie by Tamara Wellons on Apple Music – https://music.apple.com/us/album/songs-for-janie/526816507

4   Unemployed Blues – https://www.youtube.com/watch?v=vE7-AsmJQtE

form a band that is inspired by world music traditions, particularly Kirtan, India's ancient call-and-response form of chanting. We have adapted this music with blues, electronic sounds, and the harmonica. So, I have been both creating and performing and so have finally uncovered and displayed those hidden talents.

So, what next? Well, perhaps this next period provides opportunities for me to coalesce those elements of creativity and communication. My world music draws from a spiritual heritage. Both musical ventures and, indeed, writing this book, feed my creative soul and, beyond that, may guide a path for me and others where no path is clear now. Until then, I await the bell tolling; you got mail, that message is for me.

DEDICATIONS

I dedicate this book to my late father, who passed away just as I was finishing the book. As I remember my father's final days, I recall how from his deathbed, he mentioned his favourite passage in this book where I described jumping off the end of the boat in Brazil and hanging on for dear life lest I drop the rope and thus be left alone at sea. As we left the hospital on that final day after my father had passed, I felt that I had lost my moorings. I was alone again, as though at sea. I wondered what relevance my hometown of Sheffield would hold for me anymore.

My father was an English teacher and instilled in me a love of language. He encouraged me to complete this book and suggested I meet with the editor who lived up the road from him in Sheffield. I owe so much to my father, not least his step-by-step encouragement as he read through each of the early chapters.

I also dedicate this book to my son, who took my love of adventure and creativity but who took these traits far beyond what I had achieved in the same mid-twenties age. From becoming a millionaire in his early twenties to forging a career in music and travelling far wider than I, my son continues to inspire me.

ACKNOWLEDGEMENTS & NOTES

would like to acknowledge Mark Beaumont-Thomas who guided me through this writing by providing helpful suggestions and additions and not least careful editing in a language that I can no longer claim I fully know.

I would also like to acknowledge my brother Bernard Murphy, an accomplished author of books such as *The Tell-Tale Entrepreneur: A Guide to Storytelling in Business.* Bernard helped me with organization of some sections and kept me honest about our mischievous childhood days.

I changed some people's names to protect their privacy.